THE
FORGOTTEN
MOUNTAIN

DEDICATION

There are no words that will adequately compliment Cathy for who she is in her own right and for what she has done for me over the years. She has stayed in the shadows, raising our five sons and encouraging me so God's plan could unfold. She is the hero of the family. Only God can adequately bless her for what she has done and for who she has been...a loving, tireless, compassionate and powerful disciple of her King Jesus.

DEDICATION

I would like to dedicate this book to my wife MaryAlice. Words can't even express the love and the support you have been in everything I do. Without you none of this is possible. My love to you.

DESTINY IMAGE BOOKS BY DON NORI, SR.

God

The Voice

Supernatural Destiny

Romancing the Divine

Manifest Presence

Breaking Generational Curses

Secrets of the Most Holy Place

Secrets of the Most Holy Place Vol. 2

Tales of Brokenness

The Angel and the Judgement

You Can Pray in Tongues

The Prayer God Loves to Answer

Breaking Demonic Strongholds

So You Want to Change the World?

How to Find God's Love

God: Out of Control, Out of the Box, Out of Time

No More Sour Grapes

The Love Shack

The Hope of the Nation That Prays

The God Watchers

Morning Prayer

THE
FORGOTTEN
MOUNTAIN

The Place of Peace in
a Time of Confusion

Dr. Don Nori, Sr.
Ambassador Clyde Rivers

DESTINY IMAGE® PUBLISHERS, INC.

P.O. Box 310, Shippensburg, PA 17257-0310

"Promoting Inspired Lives."

This book and all other Destiny Image and Destiny Image Fiction books are available at Christian bookstores and distributors worldwide.

Cover design by: Eileen Rockwell

For more information on foreign distributors, call 717-532-3040.

Reach us on the Internet: www.destinyimage.com.

ISBN 13 TP: 978-0-7684-0922-2

ISBN 13 eBook: 978-0-7684-0923-9

For Worldwide Distribution, Printed in the U.S.A.

1 2 3 4 5 6 7 8 / 20 19 18 17 16

Contents

Contents

The Forgotten Mountain

The King and His Kingdom have been the passion of my life for many years. The inner governance of the King in my heart has been the topic of countless hours of prayer, meditation, and study. I may not have been sure of much over the years, but of this I was positive. True world peace, authentic tolerance, and brotherhood would only be possible when the King ruled the heart of man, trumping the cultural, religious, political, and geographic limitations with which we confine ourselves. His Kingdom was bigger than mere mortals could wrap their heads around. His love, mercy, compassion, and justice were more equitable than any man's constitution or the interpretation of any man's holy book.

I have always wanted, more than anything else in this world, to be the authentic representation of His Life in the earth. I wanted an understanding so clear that it would serve as a launching pad into the reality of the Kingdom-ruled. But for all I had written, all I had studied, there were key points missing to this journey I had committed myself too.

Then I met Dr. Myles Munroe, who I consider the father, the apostle, the pioneer of the modern Kingdom experience. We would listen to him for hours talking about what he saw of this incredible Kingdom. This was years before we published his first book on the Kingdom of God. We asked him again and again to write on it for everyone to experience. He would smile and tell us to be patient, saying that the foundations of purpose, potential, relationships, and family needed to be presented before his Kingdom message could be introduced.

It was worth the wait. His words challenged and confirmed, directed and encouraged, revealed and demonstrated the limitless wonder of the King-surrendered life.

Years passed as my understanding of the Kingdom expanded, undergirded by the books he wrote. The world would never be the same; I would never be the same. My life's course was forever changed as I discovered the joy of Divine surrender.

Nonetheless, a piece was still missing. A piece that would connect the concept of the Kingdom with the Church Jesus is building as the tangible witness of true inner governance. That piece came in the person of Ambassador Clyde Rivers. His profound understanding of 'Kings' and my understanding of 'priests' with the foundation provided by Dr. Munroe was the correct combination as provided by the great Alchemist, Who worked diligently and purposefully in our lives to bring us to now, for a time such as this. This first book is the product of three lives intertwined and interacting as only the Divine can do.

The Forgotten Mountain transcends all things earthly to establish all things Divine. It lights the way to peace, opens the heart to deeply abiding joy, and fires the imagination to the endless possibilities of accomplishment when the Mountain of the King is finally and firmly planted in the hearts of otherwise ordinary people.

There is no doubt. The Mountain of the Lord turns the ordinary into the extraordinary, the average into excellence, and hope into experiential reality.

Don, Sr.

CHAPTER ONE

The Forgotten Mountain

And it will come about in the last days that the mountain of the house of the Lord will be established as the chief of the mountains. —Micah 4:1

This is the forgotten mountain, but it will not be forgotten for long.

When the ancient prophets first peered into eternity and gazed upon the all-encompassing Mountain of Divine love, they knew the time would come when this mountain would finally become the Mountain that the nations would gladly find as their refuge and strength. These Ancients understood that the last days would see this Mountain rise to its rightful place among men. But they would have to wait for the right time that would signal the unfolding of all they saw. These faithful prophets wrote what they saw with trembling hands and their hearts bursting with the wonder of what this planet was destined to experience. Thus have their writings lived on and caused more than one mystic to search out what times or seasons eternity was indicating when these eternal words were written. But what would ultimately unfold would be far different than what mere mortal man would be able to comprehend. It would take a special people indeed to administrate such an awesome vision as the one these Ancients saw.

But it became the forgotten Mountain.

Man has marched confidently through time. He became master of the earth, master, even, of each other. People were reduced to objects for others to subdue, control, and enslave. The years turned into decades, then centuries and longer. The Mountain waited whilst man's corruption, his evil, grew with his pride. His territory and influence expanded with each unrighteous act. To be sure, humanity groaned under the weight of their oppression. Men bragged of their power. They scoffed at the warnings of "lesser men." They had become invincible, or so they thought. For in their wickedness, they enlarged their own power through trading of every luxury on the face of the earth, including the bodies and souls of men (see Rev. 18:13).

Now, as it did many times before, the earth trembles under the weight of the decadence of prideful men. It buckles under the passions of those vying for influence, control, domination. Whether secular or religious, men have looked to their own wisdom, their intellectual prowess in their pursuit of the domination they crave.

Yes, not many have seen what the Ancients saw so long ago. Not many have embraced the possibilities of this Mountain emerging onto the human scene. Nonetheless, the prophets' words are alive and as passionate as when they were first recorded by trembling hands and hearts. Once again, their words are causing awakening. Though man continues on his destructive path, oblivious to what is about to happen, the forgotten Mountain is being rediscovered and embraced for what it truly is.

And he carried me away in the Spirit to a great and high **mountain***, and showed me the great city, the holy Jerusalem, descending out of heaven from God, having the glory of God. Her light was like a most precious stone, like a jasper stone, clear as crystal* (Revelation 21:10-11 NKJV).

They shall not hurt nor destroy in all My holy mountain, for the earth shall be full of the knowledge of the Lord as the waters cover the sea (Isaiah 11:9 NKJV).

Who is ready for the fulfillment of the words of these ancient holy men?

Many leaders have judged themselves capable of bringing restoration and wholeness, harmony, and peace to humanity. They make their plans, develop their lofty goals and announce their marching orders fully intending to subdue the nations, religions, and cultures. All the while, the Mountain of the House of the Lord lies ignored, judged unnecessary, out of touch in the shadows of man's self-proclaimed greatness. But the visions of the prophets, etched on parchment so long ago, are waiting for man to come to the end of himself, to come to the terrifying realization that there are no answers, no plans, no schemes that man will ever put forth to reverse the free fall of society in these last days. In their own strength, even their political, religious, and moral strength, so eloquently spoken, the free fall to destruction is not being stopped.

Some are recognizing the failure of the very important plans of very important men attempting to do very important things for the good of all men. Some, after very careful analysis and evaluation, have the courage to admit that all that man attempted to conquer was never intended to be conquered, but rather, the intention was for man to be lovingly gathered by the King of the Mountain most have chosen to marginalize, to ignore.

Some men are turning their gaze in desperation to the Mountain once forgotten, although triumphantly detailed by the prophets who knew, without question, that this day would most certainly come. And it has come. Man is come to the precipice of emptiness, the brink of human disaster. Though others frantically work to rebuild the broken ideologies of mere mortals, shouting with more desperate words and hollow promises, there are some whose ears will no longer be tickled. Some will no longer respond to the empty words of hopeless and heartless men or be intimidated by the ruthless hatred of evil forces now unleashed on the earth.

The forgotten Mountain will not be forgotten for long.

Honest men and women are turning their hearts, their hopes, their futures over to the One who alone dwells on this once forgotten peak. The Mountain of the House of the Lord will become the chief of every mountain on earth, exactly as prophesied. But it will not rise to its rightful place because of religious frenzy or immovable orthodoxy. It cannot be legislated to the position of chief Mountain or forced to a place of authority by edict or proclamation. It cannot be voted into such a place nor can men force it into place with violence or brute force. The external plans of man, no matter how enthusiastically stated, will never transform the heart of man. For it is in the heart of man himself that the Mountain of the House of Lord has laid dormant in anticipation for a time such as this. But desperate men and women everywhere are surrendering to the King so that His Kingdom can be founded within the heart of man.

The Mountain has been obscured by the mist of human striving and the sweat of human assumption. It has been ignored over the millennia; its existence even denied. Man has been that certain of his supremacy, his dominance over the earth and all its inhabitants, even over each other.

But in these last days, global and unchecked atrocities are surely uncovering the depths of human depravity, exposing man's complete inability to govern himself. All this is in stark contrast to the majesty and wonder, the brightness and promise of the King who dwells on the Mountain of the Lord.

Some are beginning to notice. Some are no longer making excuses as our dire conditions are becoming visible to all who are willing to see. For the hope of the world is not in a new form of institutional governance, not in a new world leader with new promises that can never be fulfilled, not in new religion or in the refinement of an old one. The hope of the world is the very real work of a very real King, who is diligently focused, eternally determined, and has sacrificially showed us His way of true love.

Why Now?

This Mountain is the authority of redeemed humanity, submitted to the King of this Mountain and in the relationship of committed union, selfless transformation, eternal Union. The Mountain of the House of the Lord is within, waiting for those who die to themselves in order to see His expression through the likes of simple folks like you and me.

The forgotten Mountain is coming onto the stage of human governance and is beginning to emerge as the chief of all the mountains of authority and dominance. Having waited for man to discover his inner emptiness and bankruptcy, it is becoming visible by a most unpredictable phenomenon—genuine inner transformation. No longer will the nations be governed by those who have no inner governance to support the words they say. No longer will the people be so void of true discernment that they will not be able to hear the truth in spite of the spoken word.

The hearts of men and women are the birthplace of the Kingdom lifestyle in the earth. It is found among the most unlikely of all people. Kingdom reality is being born within the hearts of the broken turned mighty, the weak turned strong, the rejected turned powerful, the lame turned healers, the backward turned kings, the stutterers turned mighty men, the forgotten turned counselors, fools turned wise, and the mighty turned humble.

The Right Time

Contemporary humanity is much like the children of ancient Israel coming to the banks of the Jordan after forty years of wandering, failing, rebelling, deceiving, wallowing in unbelief and confusion. The old generation had finally died off, and for the first time they heard the confident words of an overcomer who saw the land of promise inhabited by enemies bigger and stronger than they. He saw the riches of the land and the risk of possessing it, yet Joshua courageously announced that the Israelites were able to go up and take the country from the Jordan River to the sea. It was a breath of fresh air, a new hope, and a determined direction after so many years of being sidetracked and sidelined by their wobbling faith and feeble obedience. The time had come. They stood at the waters of their destiny. This is where their God wanted to take them some forty years earlier. Now, they were here. On the brink of destiny they would have to decide whether they would finally respond to God or once again turn back into the wilderness where there was no hope, no direction, and certainly no destiny.

So here we are as well. We have followed many very smart men, many charismatic leaders and dedicated holy men. We have new discoveries in science, inventions to make life easier, psychological and cultural advisors to tell us what is right and wrong. After all this, we are at the end of ourselves. We have been found wanting, waning, and wandering. We are on the very brink of human disaster where we will either ignore the reality around us and plow on to our own demise or we will have the courage to face our failure, our uncertainty, our pride and admit that we need a King who will have our best interests at heart. At this most critical point in our global history, the King stands at the door of humanity's heart and He is knocking. Who will allow Him unhindered entrance, access, and dominion?

Where Does the World Turn?

Governments are desperate. They organize commissions, committees, town hall meetings. Some governments sanction research studies and others appoint czars. The results are predictably fruitless for they are still convinced that human intellect alone can solve every problem. They call good, bad and bad, good. They blur the line between the sacred and the sinful. They deny God but allow extreme zealots of every stripe to flourish, *even religious zealots*. There is barely a distinction between good and evil. All this in the hope that man can finally solve his own problems and ultimately live in harmony with one another. These vain attempts at humanistic governance and man-made policy only end in deterioration and wanton lawlessness. Society may deny it, but nature does not. Eventually nature prevails, no matter how man denies its realities. Even our greatest scientific minds cannot alter the DNA of nature itself. The further culture disintegrates, the fewer and fewer rules there are that are acceptable—of course, with the exception of the rules that keep the powers that are in control, in control. Many have shortsighted goals and have not thought through the consequences of shallow governance and policy. But these consequences are written in the very fabric of the cosmos and cannot be violated without tragic result.

Religion?

So is religion the answer? Those who claim experience, fellowship, or communication with this otherworldly dimension are often deemed unfit at worst and untrustworthy at best by most who are entrenched in the currently accepted forms of governance. If the truth be known, the religionists are as incapable of governance as the secularists. No, religion has not proven to be any better. For history is also full of awful religious wars and attitudes. Their zealots have successfully alienated the world from the One whom they so completely misrepresent.

Allowing their own fleshy zeal to consume them, they have destroyed nations on a grand scale and torn apart families on an individual scale. They have presented a most anti-Christ view of the genuine Christ of God, who in His eternal wisdom actually demonstrated that love by self-sacrifice—not by forcing others to sacrifice themselves—brings true peace. Yet even to this day, tyrannical voices continue to give air to the hatred and destruction that the King came to put an end to. These folks do not represent the reality of the loving God who gave His Son for humanity's sake that they might live a life of fulfillment, peace, and rest.

God has moved many times over the centuries and is evidenced by the number of monuments built as a result of His attempts to get the attention of mankind. Every time God begins to do something monumental, man builds a monument. A spiritual restoration begins and man constructs a monument to be admired instead of allowing true repentance to bring lasting change and the restoration the King intended. God moving within the heart is where the true transformation begins. When man claims the work of the King as his own invention, for his own purposes, that work comes to an end. The worship of the event replaces the wonder of His Presence. His formational power in the hearts and lives of man is thwarted.

What Makes This Different?

Throughout our history, most have governed or at least attempted to govern from the top down, the outside in. They have used everything from legislated policy to war and slavery in order to keep the folks in line. This outward governance ultimately fails. The heart of man is desperately evil. It cannot help but find its way to a place that it oppresses the land and the people. One can keep the evil within at bay for only a time. It will eventually show its ugly face in subjugation, guile, intimidation, control, and all the worst that the human heart can conjure.

So what makes this different? The governance of the Mountain of the House of the Lord rests in the heart of man. Here, the King does not control the actions of man; He woos them that so that He can change their hearts. This inner governance is the King Himself reigning within those who yield to Him. Men act differently under the rulership of this King because they are different. The old, self-centered ways of humanity are replaced by the will of the King and His attributes. Man no longer rules from a methodology of governance; rather, he rules from the heart, now transformed by the King. In short, the leader becomes what he teaches.

He lives the life he wants his people to live. He becomes an example of the peaceful, loving, compassionate person his governance teaches. This lifestyle is one of *broken repentance*. That is, they have come to the conclusion that they will fail without His inner transforming power. They are aware of their shortcomings, their weaknesses, and their penchant to fail Him. So they walk softly, circumspectly. They are attentive to the King and are ready to change anything that He requires. They know who they want to rule their hearts and live with an attitude of soft-heartedness and teachableness. They are taught by the King Himself and in turn broadcast to all around them His message of peace and hope in the lives they live, not just in the words they say.

But make no mistake. Meekness is not weakness. These are mighty men and women who are ambassadors of the King, and they will inherit the earth. For the King of the forgotten Mountain is now rising in the hearts of mere men. The King is becoming visible in this life, in our day, as the King of the Mountain of the House of the Lord that the Ancients wrote of so long ago and boldly spoke of as the day when the nations would stream to its light. That time has arrived. That day is now.

The Sacrificial Covenant

Enter the true kings and priests of the Mountain of the House of the Lord, those who have made a covenant with the King by sacrifice—their own sacrifice (see Ps. 50:5).

But wait. I know. We have such preconceived notions of what this will look like that most run from even the thought of it, myself included. But for all our study, for all our books and philosophies, there is a very important spiritual principle that most have missed. Simply put, without a transformation within the heart of man, everything will always go on as it has. Fortunately, there are those who have set themselves apart to the King. They see their utterly bankrupt nature apart from their Lord. They have confessed the depth and the potential of the evil within and have surrendered themselves to the only One who can save them from themselves as well as give them the privilege of serving the nations—the King of the Mountain of the Lord. They have made a sobering discovery about themselves.

They understand life apart from this Divine inner governance. They know who they are and what they are capable of apart from God and it caused them to yield their lives, their futures to Him. As a result, they have made the commitment to give themselves to Him for inner transformation, the kind of change that allows the very love and Presence of God to flow through them. They have seen and have understood His power, for they have seen His love as well as His power at work within their own hearts. But I am ahead of myself. Allow me to start at the beginning.

Fruit Proof: Beyond the Christ-centered Life

The function of kings and priests is as direct as it is simple. They allow the Life of God to flow freely through them. They display, in their own lives, the possibilities of true peace, equality of all men, and the opportunity awaiting those who will also yield to Him. The evidence of His reality in the life of an individual is what the apostle Paul calls the fruit of the Spirit. There is no argument; this evidence of a King-yielded life should be easily seen by all. Equally, there is no acceptable time when this Divine evidence should not be present. In the past, many have tried to be "Christ-centered" or "King-centered," meaning they tried to pattern their lives after the Life of Christ. They determined what He would do and studied to understand His ways. But without death to self, true King-centered life is impossible. Man must die. He must humble himself; surrender himself to the King; empty himself of his own plans, pride, and personal possibilities for his fleshy ways are certainly opposed to God. Man must ultimately rise up to resist rule from any external force, whether that be from himself, secular, or spiritual. But read on—the King does not wage wars; He establishes peace, harmony, and opportunity for all men. Those who claim the inner governance of the King do not intimidate, condemn, or create a nation of slaves in the guise of public safety or "the greater good." That is nonsense. It denies the very heart of the King whose passion has always been to bring opportunity, peace, and fulfillment to all mankind.

Come

Come, let us go up to the Mountain of the Lord. For there He will teach us of His ways that we may walk in His path, for out of Zion, the dwelling place of the King, will go forth the governance of the King, and His word will flow from the hearts of the meek and will heal the land. For the land that once mourned will flourish in the joy of the King. The people, once oppressed, will find their destiny within their own hearts, where the King establishes His Kingdom and rules with a heart of love, compassion, mercy, and peace.

There is no doubt that these words also will find their ultimate fulfillment. The only remaining question is this: "Who will give themselves to the King so that these final prophetic words will come to pass?" All they have ever said hinged upon the response of men to God, as man's free will is sacred territory before God. He will not infringe upon man's right to choose his own destiny. But these days are perilous. The hope of the world lies within the hearts of those who are of no reputation, little stature, and few endorsements—those who will simply respond to the call of the King to die to themselves to take of the Person of the King as the preeminent inner governmental force of their lives.

There is certainly a new order, which is really an old order, born in the heart of the King and proclaimed by the ancient prophets who saw this day and saw the emergence of the King through those who would surrender to Him. Rather than fear the future, the purposes of the King for this planet are about to unfold in ways that no one could have imagined.

Consider the ancient words of the prophet Daniel concerning the "the stone which was cut without hands" which struck the image of the kingdoms of this earth and broke them to pieces. "And the stone that struck the image became a great mountain and filled the whole earth" (Dan. 2:35 NKJV).

All the words of the Ancients have come to pass to this point in time. They have seen this Mountain as the hope of the world. They wrote it down. It is destined to be. Why not now? Why not through you?

CHAPTER TWO

Journey to the Inward Kingdom

We are on a journey. It is a journey that leads us directly into the King where there is new light, possibilities, and new hope. The scenery of that journey naturally changes as we go forward. Indeed, if there is no change of scenery, there is no movement. When there is no movement, there is no real journey. We thought we were looking for a city made without hands, whose builder and maker is God. We soon discovered that that city is us wherein are the streets of God, where there is no darkness, where the King dwells in plain sight to all who can truly see. Now we know that He alone is the quest, the prize whose ultimate union results in purpose and destiny now, in this life. Now, ours is a journey to discover the wonders of this Divine union right now. It is a journey that requires a depth of brokenness that covets personal instruction and clarification of everything that will enhance union with Him. It is hungry enough, desperate enough for the sovereign rule of the King within to make any adjustments necessary to see His reign established within.

Genuine revelation will change the heart, not just the words. Sober, prophetic insight is necessary to see the pitfalls as well as the possibilities, the limits and the unimagined, the cost and the joy of what the King is saying. The heart of the broken is detected by the passion, desire, and willingness to make the turn in the road when our spiritual GPS tells us to, in spite of how vehemently we have resisted change in the past. This is the pattern of growth, of progress, of the way to maturity, the joy of union with God.

Going Forward

Our challenge is the challenge to every generation of believers. Will we walk the way of one on a journey of purpose or the way of walking in tradition and history? For if history has taught us anything, it has taught that history repeats itself to its own doom. Before humanity is an open door. Who will have the courage to walk through?

To condemn, to marginalize, to resist what God did through dedicated men and women in the past is to miserably miss the mark. But it is equally unacceptable to resist the growth that is the result of new understanding and vision. Historically, those with revelation resist and even condemn those with new light. But the opposite is also true. Those with new understanding condemn and ridicule what has gone before them, oblivious to the reality that it was, indeed, the patterns of the past that set up the new things God wants to reveal in our never-ending growth into the image of God. It is unfortunate, with all we have seen, heard, handled, touched of the words of Life, we still want to proclaim ourselves the kings of our own kingdoms. This is a truly fleshy pattern of pouting and arrogant religion that starts pure but ends when we discover that we are not the beginning, the end, or the whole. We are a part, nothing more and nothing less. To embrace this truth is to embrace the first major step in the inner governance of Spirit we all desire. It would be best if this pattern in our history would be finally broken in this generation. It takes true humility to understand that even when one does not agree with what came before, it is nonetheless true that yesterday paved the way to the roads of today. To marginalize what was is to open yourself to the kind of corrosive judgment that you mindlessly pronounce upon others.

This is a rebuke to the new and a warning to the old. One cannot have validity without the other. It was the old that paved the way to for the new, whether positive or negative. It is the new that validates the old. The foot cannot say to the knee, "I no longer need you." The knee cannot say to the foot, "I am complete in myself and you are not necessary." One does not move forward without the other.

Kingdom Citizens

Touring a grand cathedral in Rome late one night, Cathy and I marveled at the beauty and exquisite intricacy of each handmade window. My host smiled when he watched us marvel over such unmatched beauty. "You need to return to this place tomorrow when the sun shines through these windows. The artificial lights do not do these windows justice." He was right. There was a startling difference the next morning when we returned and the sun shone brilliantly through the windows. There was no comparison. The artificial light of the night before was nothing compared to the spectacular brilliance of the sun shining through the glass.

Of course, the same is true with us. The Son shining through us individually, uniquely, completely creates an atmosphere of Divine love, peace, and hope that "trying to be like Jesus" cannot match. We never lose our uniqueness in union with God. But those who glow with His light rather than their own artificially construed goodness are an earthly manifestation of the King's true essence. The difference between the two is, well, it's like the difference between night and day. For we are transferred from the domain of darkness into the Kingdom of His beloved Son.

But the nearness of God is not a flippant experience, nor is it safe for the deceptive of heart. His reality within changes everything. He is suddenly not a philosophy, not a doctrine or a belief system. Suddenly, and I do mean suddenly, He is the living Creator God who has come to dwell within the human heart—yours and mine. Ancient Israel was happy to have God on Mount Sinai. He was far away from those who called Him God. They did not have to deal with the immediacy of His Presence. He was a safe distance for their human antics. But David brought the Presence back to the people.

He pitched a tent, as it were, in his backyard for the Presence of the King to dwell. The Divine was now there, near, immediate.

David's tabernacle is a type of man's heart. It is the ultimate dwelling place of the King that He determined would be His own dwelling place forever. This is where the reality of God interacts with the heart of man. Having a person's life centered in the King is not the same as having the King rule freely through him. This is what King David saw as he peered through the ages to the end times and spoke the words of God:

> *For the Lord hath chosen Zion* [us]; *he hath desired it for his habitation. This is my rest for ever: here will I dwell; for I have desired it. I will abundantly bless her provision: I will satisfy her poor with bread. I will also clothe her priests with salvation: and her saints shall shout aloud for joy. There will I make the horn of David to bud: I have ordained a lamp for mine anointed* (Psalm 132:13–17 KJV).

When the King rules the heart, He does things that are unconventional, unrecognizable, and certainly unacceptable to the natural order of life as it was commonly accepted. Yes, He walked in great compassion and love to the oppressed, but He also spoke out against the man-centered religious governance. He was not afraid to call them out as those leaders ruled the people with humanly contrived laws and traditions. To be sure, the systems of men filled the coffers of the institutions, but those same systems also left the hearts of the people empty and longing for their King.

When the King is near—rather, when the King rules—things are put back into Divine order, His order. The King expresses Himself in ways that require heart change before any real external change can be accomplished. Yes, when the King truly reigns, things change. Everything is turned upside down. Systems are broken down; authority is redefined; the land is healed; and prosperity is restored in body, soul, and spirit. In short, everything is transformed. The first become last and the last, first. Leaders become servants and servants become leaders. To live, one understands he must first die. To be truly wealthy, it becomes clear that you must first give away all you have. Life becomes noble, fulfilling, hopeful, refreshing, full of peace and inner contentment. The journey is simplified. God rules from the Mountain of the House of the Lord—us. Then all other mountains and hills can be successfully ruled for His glory, with His glory, and for the glory of all mankind. The God-intended success of the Mountain of the House of the Lord is at the door. He must first reign in the heart. The King must first establish His governance within.

Another Mountain

There is another mountain that needs to be considered. It is the mountain that holds the secret to the success of any vision one might hold dear. The governance of the Mountain of the House of the Lord is purposeful, engaged. It is focused and ready. We have spoken of His Kingdom for many years. We have grown in our understanding of its purpose, its power, and its plan. We have discovered that He will use humanity to see His Kingdom planted, grow, and flourish. But it will not be just any man or group of men. It will be established in the hearts of the yielded, the broken, the humble. The King— who describes His Kingdom as within, unseen, yet recognized by the righteousness, peace, and joy of the heart—is about to take the next step. His Kingdom will be seen among men and women who have known *no* other goal, no other desire but to see the King magnified to a desperate and hungry world.

One thing is certain, the Mountain of the House of the Lord will become the chief of all the mountains and hills on the earth. It is the Mountain of ultimate authority and consistent growth. It is the go-to destination for those seeking Divine love, inner fulfillment, and personal destiny. It does not rely on the obedience of those who would approach it. Jesus's required obedience only serves to further frustrate the believer. This is as He intended, for not even obedience is possible apart from a heart change. And heart change is brought about by the death to self so Divine Life can rule. Divine inner governance requires more than Christ-centeredness. It require death—death of self so that the authority of the Life of the King can truly dominate in the human heart.

Home of Divine Everything

The Mountain of the House of the Lord is the ultimate source of Divine love, Kingly governance, and peace. It is remarkable that He has entrusted this place of ambassador-kingship to the hearts of men and women. But then, those who respond to Him are those who have paid the price in the past and are yet willing to pay the price for this Divine inner governance. They live knowing that as the death of self works in them, the Life of the resurrected King works through them to the world. For Life to continually flow, death must continually be occurring. The prophet of the King summed it up beautifully with these words, "He must increase, but I must decrease" (John 3:30). Without Divine inner governance, man is limited to what he can accomplish and his generational influence is diminished. This is not an indictment on a person's work; it is a reality of doing the work of the Lord apart from the inner governance of the King. It is foundationally weak, inherently flawed. The purpose of the Lord since the beginning was for His rule and reign to begin first in the hearts of humanity. Speaking through the Ancients, God said, "It will come about in the last days that the mountain of the house of the Lord will be established as the chief of the mountains" (Mic. 4:1).

The sons of Zebedee wanted their seats with the King in His Kingdom. His response to them is the same response He gives to all who covet position and power apart from death. The truth is sobering, but its reality fires the heart with the possibility of walking with the King Himself. Our Divine Monarch assures us that though death comes daily, so does life here on this earth and for eternity. For the Kingdom citizen, there is but one door—the King Himself. Follow Him to death that you might follow Him in resurrection where He reigns in the heart of man.

Then the mother of the sons of Zebedee came to Jesus with her sons, bowing down and making a request of Him. And He said to her, "What do you wish?" She said to Him, "Command that in Your kingdom these two sons of mine may sit one on Your right and one on Your left." But Jesus answered, "You do not know what you are asking. Are you able to drink the cup that I am about to drink?" They said to Him, "We are able." He said to them, "My cup you shall drink; but to sit on My right and on My left, this is not Mine to give, but it is for those for whom it has been prepared by My Father" (Matthew 20:20–23).

Assured Domination

This is the term to describe the goal of the religious and secularists to secure their rule and authority generationally. Their plan is generational—modest gains in smaller time frames. The control of education, media, entertainment, and religion makes it easier to keep their ideology embedded in the hearts and minds of the population.

Religion and government carry their own agendas. Their goal is to assure their control over the generations to come. Of course, it follows that they have very little to do with the desires of the King. Their plans may or may not be in the best interests of the people under their governance. The overriding goal of these human institutions is the perpetuation of their societal control. They see their responsibility as maintaining the systems of which they are the ruling class. After all, they have determined that their existence and control are for the common good. They even use principles taken from the Holy Writ as they deem them important.

But it is their very humanity, their intellectualism, which they lean on for the rules by which society is maintained, that disqualifies these man-made institutions. They function apart from the reality of the King. Whether secular or religious, it is the absence of the living King's inner governance that makes their attempts to create policy and govern to the good of all men quite impossible. They matter-of-factly dismiss His influence on the people and ultimately the culture.

In many cases, they even deny the very reality of a spiritual world. Secularists and religionists follow the path of "assured domination," justifying whatever is necessary to insure their control over individuals as well as nations over the long term. They have no confidence in who they call the common man. They see the general population possessing neither the intelligence to rule nor the wisdom to understand the complexities of governance. Thus the spurious methods of these self-appointed guardians of humanity, however regarded, are excused as necessary for the good of the people who cannot govern themselves.

The fruit of this prevailing attitude belies the trust that so many have placed in it. There are precious few places where true intellectual governance has produced an environment of genuine peace, prosperity, and hope from generation to generation. From the very first book of Scripture to the latest current events of any news outlet, it has been proven that any form of human governance, on its own, cannot be sustained over the long haul. The world, under the control of these secularists/religionists, has tended toward decay, loss, disintegration. The evidence is overwhelming everywhere one looks. But this prevailing attitude has been so entrenched in societies around the world that the thought of anything different is looked upon as ludicrous. After thousands of years of failure, history records a sobering litany of a far more accurate perspective. It chronicles the reality of oppression, slavery, starvation, war, and death. Man's inhumanity to man knows no low as with each passing year, his God-vacant villainy finds new ways to plant true terror in his fellow man. Even some of the most dedicated idealists of the past have ironically produced the very results they wished to eradicate.

At some point, man must come to the realization that there is something more fundamental that must be understood, that must be studied. For unless the heart of a man is changed, he cannot possibly do what is necessary to bring true harmony and peace among individuals or nations. The actions of the heart cannot be legislated. It cannot be controlled by an external policy and still bring peace. The heart itself must be changed.

This issue cannot be legislated by political correctness or cultural expediency. The most powerful voices are often wrong and the money players pour their millions with little discernment and even less deep, personal conviction. To change the words of the King for sake of a false sense of inclusion and humanistic tolerance is the oil that has put this planet on the downward spiral of moral decadence. The removal of a principled compass of human behavior that has kept this world relatively balanced, however tenuous that balance has been, leaves society groping for balance and stability. The King is not pressured by such unaccountable behavior that winks at sin, ignores true justice, and bends to the fleshy cries of those who have no ethical foundation or moral plumb line. It is the personal responsibility of every human being to acquire the only stability that can rescue all of us. That stability is found only in the Mountain of the House of the Lord and the authentic inner governance it brings to the human heart.

Kingdom Snap Shot

Folks who are Kingdom citizens have come to the painful conclusion that any trust in humanity, even redeemed humanity, is misplaced. Man must be transformed. Although it is the tendency of modern man to transform the King into one of their own liking, One who will allow the fleshy antics of a self-centered, self-gratifying lifestyle, it is not His intention. It is not man who determines the ways of the King. It is the King who determines the ways of man. This is the only way for the King to truly govern the heart. One must die for the will of the other to flourish. Unless man dies to himself, the King will never rule within the heart. Instead, we will always be plagued with man assigning fleshy attributes of this dimension to the King whose attributes are from a higher dimension of life.

The certainty of success must flow from the certainty of the King. It is a reality that cannot be imitated. It cannot be legislated and certainly cannot be bought by money, favors, title, or advancement. In His Kingdom, the days of smoke-filled backroom deals are over. All things are done in the Light of His Presence and will be shouted from the housetops. The fruit proof of this mighty court of the King is the fruit of the King. There is no duality in life, ministry, or governance. These folks are the same in business, political, cultural, and family governance. Indeed, they have discovered that there is only one Life worth living—His. There is only the King, recognized by the mighty reality of love living dynamically through His subjects. He has made them as uniquely as an artist designs a stained glass window, and He shines uniquely through them for all the world to see.

Many of the Ancients have seen this King and His rule. They present compelling visuals of life in this Kingdom that is rooted within the hearts of so-called "average" folks who truly are men and women of whom the world is not worthy. Consider the prophet Isaiah who peered into the realm of Spirit, bypassing time and space to see into these last days. His visuals prove the flourishing Life the King plants in humanity.

> *Encourage the exhausted, and strengthen the feeble. Say to those with anxious heart, "Take courage, fear not. Behold, your God will come with vengeance; the recompense of God will come, but He will save you." Then the eyes of the blind will be opened and the ears of the deaf will be unstopped. Then the lame will leap like a deer, and the tongue of the mute will shout for joy. For waters will break forth in the wilderness and streams in the desert. The scorched land will become a pool and the thirsty ground springs of water* (Isaiah 35:3-7).

These words are not for heaven, the millennium, or some future new earth. These words are for now. Those with little faith have pushed these powerful promises into the future, where man is not responsible for their fulfillment. Here is the good news, the certain reality, the intent of the Divine. The benevolent rule of the King is for this life, you and I, the nations of the world; and it is absolutely attainable, livable, and most certainly experiential right now. Our responsibility is to surrender ourselves, including but not limited to our politics, our opinions, our desires, our preferences, our secret lusts, our private wanton passions and our personal agenda for our own exaltation to the King who will transform human inadequacies into the vibrant, loving, healing capacity that is the Kingdom within.

The world cannot help but change when the hearts of men and women change. Compassion, mercy, and forgiveness give way to hope as the King moves the heart to restore self-respect to those among us who are most vulnerable, at risk. Society, as a whole and under the leadership of the King, embraces the mission of well-being to all the people of the earth. As folks surrender to the King, the reality of His love to the earth is manifest in real-time actions that bring health, dignity, responsibility, and destiny to all mankind. This is not a religious agenda. It is not a political agenda. It is the agenda of the King of the Mountain of the House of the Lord whose beauty is yet to unfold among men. The world and its myriad systems have failed us. We are lost, without hope. Yet we continue to stubbornly cling to the very things that fail. Conservatives blame liberals. Liberals blame conservatives. Socialists blame capitalists. Capitalists blame socialists. Religion blames other religions. I blame you and you blame me. Citizens condemn governments and governments blame everyone. There is no end to accusation because there is no end to failure. Man is willing to scrutinize everything and everyone around him. Unfortunately, he is unwilling to admit the ugly truth that it is his own heart that needs to be scrutinized. Each one of us needs to allow the light of eternity to explore the depths of his own depravity, soberly allowing truth to invade his own heart. It is a compelling but heartrending reality. It not the rest of the world that needs the inner governance of the King, it is me.

But, thank God, I am safe in my own world, approved by my own group and certain of my own pious system of beliefs, actions, and judgments. No, the world will not change whilst we remain isolated in the tower of our own loftiness, assured of our righteousness and pitying those who have not yet been enlightened. "Come, Lord Jesus!" some shout. All the while our lives are so full of ourselves and the certainty of our beliefs that there is not room for Jesus anywhere in our world of pretentious self-assurance. So the real prayer must be, "Come, Lord Jesus, and clean up this old house that the King might find rest in my heart."

CHAPTER THREE

The King Within

Who may ascend into the hill of the Lord? Or who may stand in His holy place? He who has clean hands and a pure heart, who has not lifted up his soul to an idol, nor sworn deceitfully.
—Psalm 24:3-4 NKJV

I have climbed many mountains in my day. I have worked myself into quite a sweat as I have attempted to reach the top of some high places that were quite coveted indeed. I climbed with expectations high and innocence real. I climbed with determination and hope, with certainty and plenty of delusions of grandeur. There were many who had gone before me over the same trail. I had heard their tales of wonder and accomplishment, of adventure and discovery, heartache and trial. "Certainly," I imagined, "if others have made the trek to the great heights of these formidable mountains, so can I." You would think that I would have noticed how the roadway was so well worn, obviously by the myriad of those who had gone before me. But no, with eyes wide shut and my heart engaged in a hopeless case of naiveté, I went on, so sure the reward would be worth the troubles and sacrifice in getting there. I knew I could do it; I knew I had what it took to dominate any mountain I had decided to climb. With God's help, I could do anything.

But if the truth be told, I really didn't want God's interference; I only wanted His help in getting there. I was interested in seeing Him removing the obstacles along the way—the people, the processes, the laws, the struggle. If God could remove all my troubles and finance it along the way, I would have truly arrived, or so I believed. The fact is, I really thought I wanted what He wanted for me.

In those days, I didn't realize that the Mountain of the House of Lord was anything I had to be concerned with. Neither did I understand that fulfilling destiny would cost me everything. I thought that was a given. I soon made a few startling discoveries. First, the primary mountain that I had to deal with was the Mountain of the House of the Lord. That mountain was within my heart.

The government of the Mountain of the House of the Lord was nothing like I had envisioned. The King was not impressed with my prayers, asking, begging, demanding that He help me achieve my dream. Oh, He wants me to fulfill a dream, but He is interested in His owns dreams, through me, if I was so inclined to allow Him. I had yet to learn that His dreams were the very dreams that would bring me the peace, the fulfillment, the love that I so deeply wanted. I had to learn that His dreams for me are eternal; mine are temporal. His dreams bring wholeness to the nations. My dreams bring attention to me.

Sure, He would help me. He would bless me, teach me, provide for me because I am His child. But His ultimate intention is to have those who will allow Him to establish His governance within their hearts. This King wanted more than I understood. He wanted me. He wanted to use me as His beachhead in establishing His Kingdom on this planet. I would see wonders beyond my imagination, and I would experience a fellowship with the King that others only dream about. The best I had going for me was that the yearning of my heart was out of my control. My heart ached for Him, for His Life, His love within. But this King does not show favorites. He moves on us all equally, drawing us all to His inner dwelling place, our hearts, where we experience true union with the Divine.

So I made the decision. I would seek out this Mountain. I would explore its wonders, study its possibilities, surrender myself to this spiritual union with the King and then watch what He would do. I would give myself, die to myself, and live to Him. What I discovered would change my life forever. I was about to be moved from the kingdom of darkness to the Kingdom of the Beloved King. I was about to change my citizenship—not in word, not in doctrine but in amazing, fulfilling reality.

Mountains and Hills

The Bible has always referred to "mountains" and "hills" as strongholds or places of authority and dominance. This theme is a prominent thread throughout the Scriptures. A mountain is a place of authority and power, union and communication, strength and safety. Noah's ark rested on a mountain when the waters subsided. It was the symbolic declaration of the authority of God over the earth. Moses received the Ten Commandments on a mountain called Sinai, for all law and governance must flow from Him. The Tent of Meeting, which housed the Ark of the Covenant and the very Presence of God, was on Mt. Gibeon. Here man had to look up; he had to climb the mountain of His authority to commune with God. David's Tabernacle, where King David placed the Ark of the Covenant, was on Mount Zion. Here man found that the Mountain of the Lord was within reach; that God would, given the opportunity, dwell within, planting His Kingdom inside the heart of man; that God's authority was established on the earth when it is established in man. King Solomon built the mighty temple as directed by God on the mountain called Moriah in Jerusalem. Here, the glory of God would be seen by nations who are destined to stream to His Light. Jesus often went into the mountains to pray. He went to the place of symbolic authority, for man's sake, to hear from His Father. He was crucified on the hill of Calvary typologically showing even the crucifixion of His Son was under the authority of God.

Many Mountains

Mountains are a dynamic type, a shadow of authority. Mountains are strong, immovable, formidable. They represent permanence, power, protection. There is little wonder, then, that the ancient prophets use this profound symbolism when they prophetically declare the events of the Last Days, the very days we find ourselves in now. They saw governments, religions, philosophies, and movements. They saw men lifting themselves up as gods on the high places, claiming the authority of the times while usurping the authority of the King as though the King had no place in their earthly affairs.

It is not that some are not well-intentioned. Certainly there are those leaders on every mountain who may have the best interests of the people at heart. But man cannot maintain even his own high ideals and moral standards. Man needs the strength of the Mountain of the Lord to bring about what is best for himself and for those around him. Unfortunately, it is difficult for man to see his own lack, his barrenness, his desperate need of the strength required. He just stumbles on or arrogantly and blindly struts on, ignoring the obvious whilst making the same mistakes he has made for thousands of years.

Yet, God had made these leaders. He loved them. He knew all about them. He knew their frailty. He understood their limitations. To be sure, He gave them the Ten Commandments to show them their utter inability to make right decisions on their own, to show them their weakness to follow any moral standard or to care for the needs of all those less fortunate. More than just a list of God's most important rules, the Ten Commandments were to show man his desperate need for an authority greater than himself who would rescue man from himself. For humanity had run amuck in establishing its own mountains, its own high places of authority and rulership. Year after year, decade after decade, century after century, millennia following millennia, man has proven that he cannot govern righteously over the long haul. A man's beginnings may be strong, but he has no permanent moral foundation to carry his dream to fulfillment, no matter how noble his intentions.

Our Constitution was made only for a moral and religious people. It is wholly inadequate to the government of any other. —John Adams

Man needs more than a list of the right things to do; he needs a King. He needs a King who will reign righteously, love unconditionally, rule with justice and equity. This is the King who has every intention to reign first within the heart of man. The King understands that the only hope of success that man has is to be ruled by One who has already conquered death, human passion, and the enemy himself.

Let us not forget that the King faced the enemies of His soul and He won. He overcame. He destroyed the power of His enemy and ours. It is fitting, then, that the conquering King take up residence within, establishing His victorious Kingdom in our hearts as well. He has already won the war, not just a battle. Surrendering to the One who is victorious, aligning our hearts to His, makes His victory ours.

So it follows that at some point, the wise and discerning would see the futility of their kingless society—to be sure, the futility of their kingless lives. They would come to the profound realization that they could not, cannot, and will never be able rule with the selfless love and compassion that the King had intended. Man would be forced to admit to himself that he needs a King greater than himself. If he wanted to succeed in the most profound sense, if he wanted lasting peace within and without, he would, of necessity, submit to the rule of the King. He would find he must embrace this King and His ways if he was ever going to come to the place of peace and wholeness in this life. He must surrender his personal control to the King.

Whether man's rule was over himself, his family, his work, or his government, the righteous One would need to set up His kingly rule within so that man might experience the joy and fullness the King had intended for him. Man would have to surrender control to the King within him, so that he might truly reign in righteous equity, true compassion, and Divine love. It is a conundrum only when there is no wisdom. For man to live, he must die. For him to rule, he must lay down his own authority. For him to reign, he must serve. He would need inner governance to the core of his being before the Life of the King would flow so effortlessly through him.

The rule of the King in the heart of a person is the hope, the joy, the future of those over whom He reigns.

When the righteous are in authority, the people rejoice: but when the wicked beareth rule, the people mourn (Proverbs 29:2 KJV).

The Work of the King

His work does not begin with governance of the world. He does not lobby legislative bodies or control international organizations. The work of the King is established in the place of secret fellowship, where very personal, continuing transformation of the inner man takes place; where lasting governance is rooted and grows into a world-engulfing reality of true peace among men. This King rules from the heart of man where truly Divine love is resident, nurtured, and poured out on all of mankind.

The Mountain of the House of the Lord is biblical symbolism for the place where the King is planting His Kingdom. It is not only where He dwells; it is where He has established His permanent home. From this mountain shines the light that is the brightness and glory of the King, the hope of the world. It represents the unmovable truth of God's love and the never-changing expression of that love. It is, to be sure, the place of His Divine governance, the proof of the victorious nature of His reign in man. But His Divine influence is not confined there; it only begins there. It's influence reaches the four corners of the earth and becomes the focal point of all who want to see Him and experience the harmony, the love, the peace that He has established on His mountain.

Divine Intent

The ancient prophets cried out in prophetic unison to all men, declaring with pinpoint accuracy the determined heart of the King. Though man arrogantly goes about fulfilling his own desires, his own plans, seemingly unaware of a better way, the prophets cement in time and space what is already cemented in the heart of the King Himself. With joyful anticipation, they deliver the purposes of God that should be music, hope, and anticipation to hearts of man. The King is coming…through you.

> *Now it will come about that in the last days the mountain of the house of the Lord will be established as the chief of the mountains, and will be raised above the hills; and all the nations will stream to it* (Isaiah 2:2).

Mankind does not have to do it alone. The truth is, they were never intended to have to do it alone. God had intended from the very beginning to set His King on the Mountain of the House of the Lord, from which His rule and authority, both in heaven and earth, flow. Man has the option, as he always does, to continue on his treacherous path of self-rule and self-government, truly expecting that someday, if he does it often enough, says it convincingly, he will get it right. But of course, Einstein was right, "stupidity" is doing the same thing whilst expecting a different outcome. Sometimes our arrogance is appalling.

Who Sees the King?

Men will always struggle for authority, for dominance. They struggle over which of the mountains will be the chief of all the mountains. Men vie for this authority. Nations and governments are displaying their potency. Philosophies, dogmas, declarations, and religions are clamoring for their place of ultimate rulership. Folks are sacrificing everything for their shot at universal control. They want to occupy, to rule the mountains and the hills, to stake their claim as chief of the highest mountain.

But alas, that ultimate mountain is already occupied. It is controlled by One who has been there since before the beginning, for He Himself created the mountain He occupies. It is an amazing mountain indeed. It is the only safe, fulfilling, and compassionate gathering place of humanity. It is where man forfeits his claims. It is where he lays down his passions, his cravings in order to live in a place of true rest and peace.

For the King rules with peace. His overriding motivation in all He does is love. He rules with Divine, compassionate, healing, restorative love. Here, man can truly rest. He can safely have another in control. Man can live in the confident assurance that this King has humanity's best interests at heart. The fulfillment of the King is in the peace and wholeness of the people in His Kingdom. The difference between righteous rule and the rule of man is clear. Whether one stands atop the mountain in his home, his business, his religious organization, his city, or his country, the Mountain of the King's habitation is always the plumb line.

> *Who among you is wise and understanding? Let him show by his good behavior his deeds in the gentleness of wisdom. But if you have bitter jealousy and selfish ambition in your heart, do not be arrogant and so lie against the truth. This wisdom is not that which comes down from above, but is earthly, natural, demonic. For where jealousy and selfish ambition exist, there is disorder and every evil thing. But the wisdom from above is first pure, then peaceable, gentle, reasonable, full of mercy and good fruits, unwavering, without hypocrisy. And the seed whose fruit is righteousness is sown in peace by those who make peace* (James 3:13–18).

The Mountain of the House of the Lord is far above all principality and power, above all things visible and invisible, all things contrived and concealed. Let's say this clearly. The Mountain of the House of the Lord, in the realm of Spirit, is where truth is clear and authority undisputed. It *is* the chief of all the mountains. Whether there are seven mountains or seven hundred mountains, *this* mountain, the mountain where He alone rules, He alone is King, shines with a beacon that sheds light and life on all other places of authority. There has never been a mountain quite like this mountain, nor will there ever be again.

Evidence of Kingly Rule

Every successful leader follows a system of governance. He decides what is best for the people and creates the policy that is intended to keep the country stable and the people in peace. Of course, a system that gives true peace, prosperity, and opportunity is a system that the people want and should be the final goal of every leader. No kingdom can hope to survive for long when base human instincts are the foundation of its monarchy. History has proven again and again that there is no human institution that can survive for long where human selfishness, greed, and lust are the forces behind the policy of that nation or any position of authority. No, is it not possible to simply legislate these wanton desires out of a nation or a government. Time does not permit a deep review of the results of such vain attempts to control the will of man. The sword begets the sword, domination begets greater domination, and oppression begets rebellion in the worst imaginable scenarios of human suffering.

Mankind has left a legacy of pain, destruction, the complete disregard for human life and decency as he muddled through time in his own wisdom, his own strength. His mere mortal attempts to govern have left countless millions in poverty, endless grief, and totalitarian oppression. But these godless, morally bankrupt governments rise only to fall under the weight of their own personal depravity. Though man has made endless attempts to separate the rule of government from one's personal life choices, the record shows that they cannot be separated. Of course, it is more expedient to point the finger at nations. Unfortunately, this kind of failure is evident anywhere man rules another without the inner governance of the King established within his heart.

Man's inhumanity to man is rooted in the decadence of his heart. Man cannot ultimately control himself. Sin begets destruction. The destruction of moral, ethical, legal foundations results in the ruthless control of man. The oppressed have no choice to resist and break out of the controlled systems of those who crave dominance and rulership. Many have never understood that the human spirit cannot be contained, controlled, or dominated over the long term. The very essence of the human spirit is one of exploration, discovery, and a personal quest for excellence. Those who are surrendering to the King understand the heart of the King. The King's policy creates an atmosphere that encourages every man's gift to flourish to the growth and well-being of the entire planet. His passion is to see man achieve excellence in body, soul, and spirit.

There is no doubt that this is the environment in which a man's entire being thrives, succeeds, and accomplishes more than any one person can envision. This is the path of development for which the human race was designed to bloom, prosper, and most certainly become whatever has been imagined in the heart of the King.

What Have We Missed?

The Mountain of the King is a Kingdom without borders. It has no geography to protect save the hearts of those who comprise it. There is no written citizenship save the words of the King written upon the hearts of His citizenry. But the evidence of citizenship is clearly recognizable by the uninterrupted reality of the King's Life from the heart. The Presence of the King within is the only requirement of citizenship. These folks are not citizens by decree. They carry the passion of the King's heart. They are not recognized by personal proclamation. Their citizenship is evident by their "becoming," by their "being," their daily surrender. For these folks have embodied the King. They have personally, individually relinquished their will to His. The Bible calls this process the death to self. It is in this death to self that true inner governance emerges from His citizens, for that is where it has originated.

No Confusion

Do not confuse this Mountain with a kingdom made with human hands. Do not assume that this Mountain can be governed by the rules of traditional governmental engagement, doctrines of a system, or a dominant personality. Every mountain of authority—from national government to the small business, from the international media to a personal blog, from a culture center to the home—will ultimately be successful over the long term when the King has established His governance within the human heart. Without it, man's rule is doomed to fail over the long term, as history proves.

Do not think this Mountain is a religious institution or a place for only those who think like you. It is neither religious nor secular. Is neither a western cultural movement nor an eastern religious initiative. It is eternal in nature and passes from eternity into time and space by humble, faithful, and passionate folks just like you who have committed themselves to the betterment of all mankind without religious, ethnic, political, cultural, or government prejudice.

The missing ingredient has always been the rule and reign of the King within the heart. This inner governance trumps the ways of man and begins the construction of His Kingdom within them and then without, to the world around them. Every governmental form is top down. It cannot last. The Kingdom which is established in the heart and flows from the heart changes the heart and transforms that person into a priest of the Presence before God and a king before man. The authority of this Mountain must be securely planted in us before we can rule any other mountain.

Man has been driven by his own lust for position, power, and recognition, recklessly blurring the line between all that is human and all that is Divine. We have paid an awful price for our careless lunge in our quest for personal immortality. Man has convinced himself that he is the master of his own fate, the captain of his own soul, that he alone knows what is best, that he himself is indeed god. Overpowered by his own inner turmoil, man has gone on as though there is no God, or if there is a God, He certainly cares little for humanity or the earth He supposedly created. Man refuses personal responsibility for what he has done to his fellow human being and his planet. He refuses to acknowledge his own bankrupt nature and his own runaway need for dominance and control. Man's way of doing things is to do what he wants and then blame God when it fails. Of course, this is typical for the unregenerated heart, and it leaves man faultless.

The discerning will see this as stark contrast to the healing atmosphere that is created by the Mountain of the House of the Lord.

The Law?

"Out of Zion shall go forth the law and the word of the Lord from Jerusalem" (see Isa. 2:3 KJV). The law of the Kingdom is the law that goes forth from the mountain of the House of the Lord. This law results in the fruit of His Kingdom rule. They are what you would expect to come from a King whose desire is to impart all He is to the human heart. Love, joy, peace, patience, gentleness, goodness, meekness, self-control, and confident faith, wisdom, compassion, and mercy are the exclusive by-products of true inner governance of the King.

In this observation alone, the difference between secular government, religion, moral codes on the one hand and the Mountain of the Lord on the other hand becomes undeniable and clear. The former want outward conformity whilst the King transforms the heart. Outward conformity lasts only for a season until the rage of self can no longer be imprisoned in the heart. Then, the real "you" is discovered. When the heart is authentically changed, we are at peace and the rage of our humanity can no longer rule us for it has died. We don't seem to get it.

Genuine Change

When the King changes the heart, it is changed indeed. Even when the attributes—the fruit, as it were—of the Kingdom are found lacking, the citizen of this Kingdom is teachable, pliable, soft. He knows in the deepest part of his heart that the first rule of this King is humility, daily brokenness, and change. If my actions, words, attitudes, governance does not build, encourage, release, forgive, strengthen, transform, it is not the fruit of the King.

This is contrary to so many who claim they are doing the work of God, demonstrating that so-called rule with oppression, control, intimidation, and worse, belying every word we say, every promise we proclaim, every prayer we pray. The King demonstrated His unique rulership style as He walked the earth. He healed the sick, loved the broken, and had mercy on the sinner. He gathers while others scatter; He frees while others make slaves of the people they are supposed to liberate. The King has authentic Divine love as His motivation, compassion as His plan of action. He is as opposite to what others have done in the past as up is opposite to down. His rule means true peace beginning with the heart of the individual. Once He has established a person in the Kingdom He has planted within, the fruit of that peace will affect all those within the vicinity of that peaceful heart.

Repentance Begins the Journey, Fuels the Journey

The work of the King begins when we decide that we want change. To live with Him on this Mountain requires transformation. Transformation requires death to our own ways, desires, opinions and doctrines, politics, ethnicity, and tradition. Contrary to popular belief, we are not free to believe as we wish, live as we wish, and do as we wish and still live under the authority of the King. For the King is…well, the King. He is the authority in the lives of His Kingdom citizens.

At some point, in His mercy, God will bring us to the end of ourselves. There, on the brink of human disaster, we truly begin to live as we recognize our need and repent, turning control of our lives to the control of the King for a compete redo.

There are many crossroads in our lives; each one requires a personal decision as to which direction we will go. The life of peace begins with decisions that bring peace. Most of us know right from wrong, good from evil, light from darkness. If we do not know the difference or if we deny that we know the difference, we sentence ourselves to the pain of wrong choices, shattered relationships, and unnecessary pain. But God even uses these difficult circumstances to bring us to the knowledge of right and wrong and to the place of change.

God's dream for humanity, corporately and individually, is ever on His heart. Even our wrong choices can lead us to true repentance. This is the beginning of His Kingdom within the heart. As we are attentive to His leading, prompting, conviction, and love, His rule begins to consume us quite powerfully. We may even get to the point where we say that we love to die! The prophet saw this process when he asked the question, "Who among us can live with the consuming fire? Who among us can live with continual burning?" (Isa. 33:14). The Mountain of the House of the Lord has such an incredible light shining from it that the nations will run to it.

What do you think that light is? It is the eternal light of God shining through the likes of you and me, who, having surrendered our hearts to Him, revel in the Light of His Life that shines through us to all the world. This light is the proof of a people in process, living in broken repentance, surrendering daily to the ways of the King. The light shines on the path so others may follow with the same experience of love, life and peace. To shine with His Light as a way of life, we must continue to allow Him free access to our hearts that He might show us where we need to change, to repent. We must allow Him to take everything that opposes love, mercy and compassion from our lives. The nations will stream to the genuine, the peaceful, and the trustworthy. The nations will stream to the Mountain of the Lord within the hearts of His ambassadors. The prophets have seen it. It is our destiny.

CHAPTER FOUR

Ambassadors From
Another Kingdom

Blessed are the peacemakers, for they shall be called sons of God.
—Matthew 5:9

To many believers, this verse belongs in a training manual for
the 1960s flower child movement in the US. But this verse
establishes much more than most give it credit for proclaiming.
"Blessed are the peacemakers." The world is desperate for someone,
anyone who can bring true godly peace and harmony to the world.
The King told us, "Peace I leave with you; My peace I give to you;
not as the world gives do I give to you" (John 14:27). The peace that
the King gives is not just absence of armed conflict. His peace is not
the suppression of anger, ignoring animosity, or redefining hate. His
peace is an authentic state of being as a result of inner contentment.
His peace does not react in anger, does not look for revenge, and is
seldom offended. His peace envelopes the whole person, body, soul,
and spirit, until they naturally become an agent of peace.

Yes, there are peacemakers—those who have done far more than
study the course. They have given of themselves for a cause much
greater than their own or any earthly institution or human cause.
They daily give themselves for a peace that is otherworldly in origin but very present in its expression in time and space. They have

opened their hearts to see what few have seen, risking everything for the sake of a peace that passes all intellectual engagement, all the rules of successful governance, and all the religious rhetoric that does little to genuinely affect the masses. This is the peace for which the world hungers. This the peace for which many have given their lives to either establish or protect.

Sober Decision

These emerging peacemakers are true ambassadors and have submitted themselves to the King. They have offered themselves, their hearts, their wills, their futures to the work of the King. They have voluntarily given their lives that He might set up His Kingdom, the government within their hearts. These have seen and understood that the hope of the world is not in the failed political theory of past governments and religions. There must, most certainly, be genuine inner governance of the individual heart.

The future, if it is to be the shining beacon of hope that most want it to be, will be formed by the King who has set up His Kingdom within and rules the hearts of those who not only believe in Him and in His words but actually believe Him to the point that they surrender their hearts to His Kingdom rule within, the inner governance of the heart. The folks who are the ambassadors of this Mountain believe Him to their own death to self-rule. They have relinquished self-determination for His determination for humanity. They do not mouth the words that people long to hear. These faithful men and women live the Life that the world longs to see for it is truly the King who is living His Life through them. They are becoming what they speak, what they believe, what they hope.

These are the ambassadors who will change the world. They are the peacemakers—that is, those who are committed to personal, calculated allegiance to the person of Christ, the King. He is the King and rules through the love of His Father toward His Son and all mankind. His ambassadors have discovered the answer to the question of whose plan will work and whose government will stand. They have experienced firsthand what it is to represent the King of this truly eternal Kingdom. They have seen His methods and touched His wisdom. They are in a personal transformative process that replaces the fleshy rule of selfish humanity with the selfless rule of the King. They have truly changed their allegiance and cast their lots with the One the Ancients wrote about so long ago. These are actually the days of His appearing. These are the days that will close the age. These are the people who shout to the King, "The kingdom of the world has become the kingdom of our Lord and of His Christ; and He will reign forever and ever" (Rev. 11:15).

The Dual Role of the Ambassador

The ambassadors of the King are far more than the traditional word implies. It would be a big mistake to try to define their roles in any terms that are familiar. They are far more involved, far more engaged, and far more effective than can be understood by conventional terminology. Their lives carry a peace, their voice an assurance. Their policy positions are authentic, their words are genuine, and their wisdom indisputable.

But so many have taken on the title of "ambassador," either secular or religious, with such unimpressive results. In the Mountain of the Lord, "ambassador" is more than a position. The title carries no authority, no power, no wisdom in itself. One does not simply acquire any of these qualities simply by getting the word *ambassador* placed in front of his name. Ambassadors are not appointed by man; they are appointed by the King Himself, who knows the inner working of the man's heart; understands the struggle to die to selfish ambitions; sees the purity of purpose, passion, and the moment-by-moment decision to live to the King. These are qualities in the man that will cause the King to entrust Himself to them. These are the nurturing attributes that assure that the man will yield himself to the functional purposes of the King and His Kingdom. Through folks like these, everything that the King is, in both heaven and earth, flows freely to the healing and restoration of the nations of the world.

All Mountains Are Spiritual

Ideas, philosophy, laws do not change the mountains for long. What is in the heart and what rules the heart will come out. The only hope is that the heart be changed. Of course, it is convenient to keep the heart as a separate function of life. Many of our business, governance, education, entertainment, media, religion, and family decisions are not compatible with the inner governance of the King. It is to the advantage of the unscrupulous to have a belief system that puts life components into categories that do not interfere with each other. The heart is then free to serve the King but also serve his own selfish interests.

This is but one challenge the ambassador deals with as self-serving deals, personal ambitions, and secret desires show their faces in everyday life. This is at the foundation of the ambassador's attitude, "I have died and my life is hidden in the King Whose Life is hidden in the Father of us all" (see Col. 3:3).

Accurate Representation

Now then, we are ambassadors for Christ, as though God were pleading through us: we implore you on Christ's behalf, be reconciled to God (2 Corinthians 5:20 NKJV).

True Kingdom ambassadors have one overriding responsibility in all they will do in life. They are authentic representatives of the King who has sent them because He Himself is living through them. This is difficult for our Western mindset, but it must be understood if lasting transformation will occur. We can look at the Life of the King as He walked the earth. We can see Jesus's compassion, love, and unwavering commitment to the mission for which He was sent. It goes without saying that it consumed every aspect of His Life. Today, when someone lives such a committed lifestyle, he or she is considered off-balance or worse. We have bought into that lie and the world has suffered for thousands of years because of it.

There is no doubt—authentic ambassadors are a committed lot, a sold-out company of disciples who live with the conscious awareness that the King must have His full expression through them. His will takes precedence over their own will, their own desires. Their mission is to display the love, the compassion, the mercy, the governance of the Kingdom of God within. Contrary to most opinion, this position cannot be acquired through study, cannot be purchased with money or gained by political advantage. These ambassadors become who they are by death to their own ways, surrendering their own opinions and their former political bent. The King and His ways trump everything else. This foundational point cannot be overemphasized.

There is no room for personal opinion, personal feelings, or personal advantage. The rule of the King trumps everything. Nothing can have more authority in the life of a Kingdom ambassador. The King trumps theology, politics, and their inevitable unholy alliances. They are not identifying themselves by a form of human governance, religion, ethnicity, or nationality other than their Divine citizenship. Their heart's desire is to be accurate in their representation of the King and all He represents. Notice that this is not to say that their personal ideology is just kept in check whilst they go about the business of the King. No, the former ways are gone and their new ways, the ways of the King, have been written upon their hearts. They have come to believe in the King and are now statesmen for Him and the Kingdom over which He rules. They have come to understand that their lives always represent the King. There are no vacations, no days off. Their position is not their job, it is who they have become and they are at rest, at peace with their choices.

Statesmen stand for what they believe, who they are, what they would die for. They do not bow to the winds of flippant words or passing fads. They are not swayed by money, power, or opportunity that requires a change in their belief system. They actually are what they speak. They embody their message. They are the same in public and in private. They do not have different codes of conduct according to the company they keep. Kingdom men and women are sober in their beliefs, at peace with their actions, forgiving wrongs done to them, compassionate to those in need, and loving to all men. They do not take advantage of anyone. This is who they are from the inside out. They cannot be changed, coerced, intimidated, or bought. They made a commitment to their King by sacrifice. The sacrifice they have given is themselves.

Authentic From the Heart

This comes with a price. There is only one way it can happen—they must allow Him to live His own Life through them. This is the authentic Life that the world craves. This is the Life the world is desperate to have for themselves. They are desperate for true love, for authenticity, for the King. Most do not understand that the King builds His Kingdom in the hearts and lives of everyday people. For the Kingdom is not measured in lands acquired but in hearts transformed, lives restored, love genuinely expressed.

Ambassadors of the Mountain of the Lord do not have the luxury of establishing their own identity, their own kingdoms, or ruling according to contrary personal beliefs, for they have died to them and their life is now hidden in the King who is hidden in the Father. There are no secret places in the heart, no duality of lifestyle. These folks are the same at home as they are at work. They speak the same with their family as they do with friends, colleagues, and local store clerks. To these folks, everyone is precious, everyone is loved by the King, and therefore loved by them regardless of their station in life.

Die? Really? Yes, ambassador-kings die to everything selfish and now live toward everything Kingly. Ambassador-kings must first offer themselves to the ways of the King before anyone else can be expected to do the same. When I say, "I must die," I am saying that I am the instrument of change. The change that I want around me begins with change in me. I live the change. This is the evidence of the authenticity I may claim to carry in my heart. Yes, I am the one who must change. I must die. For after death comes the glorious resurrection of Life in the earth, in me, in this life. Ambassadors of the King exchange the ways of man, no matter how deeply those ways are entrenched, to gladly embrace the ways of the King who rules within. These New Covenant ambassadors allow the King to rule freely in them and through them. They represent the King by their lives as well as their words.

This is not an easy task. Most are not really that open to change, except in someone else. To be an agent of change is to embrace the ridicule, the resistance, and the reluctance of those around you. To be an ambassador-king will require real statesmanship. A statesman holds the principles of his heart no matter how the political, cultural, or religious winds are blowing. He knows what he has seen and experienced. He knows who is in his heart and is unwavering in his confidence. As adversity grows, so does the strength to maintain the standards of his heart.

It must be that ambassador-kings become what they embrace. How can one be an ambassador of a Kingdom he has not embraced as his own? How can one speak with loyalty and authority of a King to whom he has not sworn allegiance and adopted the Life of the King as his own? The world and her systems have spoken such lofty words for so many centuries, yet few have represented their King with genuine love, authentic passion, selfless devotion.

Genuine ambassadors are governed by the King. It is evidenced by a lifestyle that is itself proof of the emerging Kingdom from within. These committed men and women live the heart of the King. The King expresses Himself through them, demonstrating statesmanship perspective with the authority, compassion, and love of the King. They are certain of their positions and cannot be deterred by any external force or influence. For they have changed. They are becoming inert to the temptations of personal advantage and the self-serving voices of others. Their heart is set because He rules the heart. Their roles are defined by the King who brings His own rules to the heart. They are motivated, happy, content, and committed to what the King builds within them. But do not think we are on our own to accomplish this inner governance of the King. Jesus sent the Holy Spirit to teach, empower, and guide us into all truth. Our King is well aware of our frailty and He has provided us with the means to fulfill our desire to be ambassadors for His Kingdom.

> *But the Helper, the Holy Spirit, whom the Father will send in My name, He will teach you all things, and bring to your remembrance all things that I said to you* (John 14:26 NKJV).

> *But when the Helper comes, whom I shall send to you from the Father, the Spirit of truth who procedes from the Father, He will testify of Me. And you will also bear witness, because you have been with Me from the beginning* (John 15:26-27 NKJV).

Two Lives

These ambassador-kings do not live two separate lives. They do not live one way in the service of the King and another way when they are alone. They are one whole person. They look the same from any direction. The inner governance of the King rules the heart or it is not true inner governance. You cannot separate the natural world from the spiritual world any more than you separate a man from his soul. They are intertwined with the intricate delicacy of a child as he is formed in his mother's womb.

Man loves to separate natural from spiritual so he can do what he wants with impunity. Whether someone owns a construction company or holds a religious title, whether a factory worker or a preacher, a governor or a schoolteacher, a stay-at-home mom or an entertainer, all activity holds profound and simultaneous natural and spiritual consequences. My life, no matter how inconsequential I perceive it to be, has eternal impact in this life and in the heavenlies.

The impact of understanding this truth is far reaching. Not only redefining my place on the planet, it redefines my impact in all my thoughts, decisions, and actions. I am not an island unto myself. The Divine has woven us inexorably together in ways we cannot yet imagine. What one would call an isolated incident affects the realm of spirit as it affects life in this dimension. Many excuse themselves of personal responsibility by keeping the two separate. They either believe their lives are unimportant in the grand scheme of things or what they do in private does not affect anyone or anything else. This is a most destructive attitude, both for themselves and for those around them. We are part of a great Divine tapestry that is wondrous indeed. Provided one is courageous enough to look beyond themselves into the glorious wonder of all we are and are created to be, he will see the grandeur of His mighty plan as well as his individual necessity to the plan.

Ambassador-kings know they are integral parts of this tapestry that is being woven by the hands of the King through them. Their role, as everyone's role is designed to be, is both Divine and natural. It is not one or the other; rather, it is a union of nature and spirit that is not completely natural and not completely Divine. It is what nature itself groans for. It is what this dimension understands is its destiny and is in travail for the true sons to be made visible on the earth.

Don't be afraid of your uniqueness. You are who you are for the purpose that the King has designed. He knows what that is and He is committed to see you thrive in that purpose. It is His commitment to you, His dream. It is His moment-by-moment guidance that will bring it about. Your moment-by-moment surrender will insure that it unfolds in its fullness with an immeasurable impact in this life and in the spirit. One thing is perfectly clear once you have seen the King. All life matters. More to the point, all life is essential, for if you are here, God has ordained it. If God ordained it, it has purpose. If you breathe, you have the potential within you to function, flourish, thrive as an ambassador of the King.

Under the Rule of the King

Ambassador Clyde Rivers had a secret dream:

"I wanted to be like Fred Price Jr. I wanted to preach like him and serve like him and help people just like he helps people."

But the King had a different plan. He had a plan for Fred Price, and He did not need me to copy what someone else was doing. The King had a separate plan for me. He wanted me to be me. He wanted me to fulfill the destiny the King had determined in His heart that was unique to me. I could not see it because I did not know my own value.

You see, until we know our own personal value we want to be someone else. But I learned that I had value through really rough times. I saw the King send me people at the right time. I heard Him speak to me just when I needed to hear Him. I saw Him get me out of circumstances that I was locked into. I had to discover that that the King personally loved me and that I had a special value in His Kingdom and a task that only I could do.

When I was in school as a young child, I didn't know what it meant to ride to school in the short bus. But as I got older, the kids around me gave me a quick education. According to them, their parents, and a whole lot of people, I was doomed to a life of failure. I would struggle to survive, have few friends and no allies. This was my future already determined in the minds of those around me. But the King had other plans. Now I am an ambassador and counselor to governments around the globe. Man saw a short bus but God saw value. He saw the dream He had placed within my heart. The world needed me to do what God had given me to do. That is the heart of the issue right now.

Anyone can see that the world is suffering, but few understand the reason why it is suffers so. When so many millions are not permitted to live to their potential, to make their God-given contribution to the earth, it is no wonder that there is such pain, such aimlessness on every continent and in every country. The aimlessness in the US is every bit as obvious as it is in Mexico, Uganda, Russia, or China. When a person's contribution is aborted, the world cannot help but suffer for it. A new way of thinking is required. A fresh perspective, a voice of hope, statesmen with real answers with a real world view of the value and necessity of every human being.

Humanity's New Paradigm

The King needs you too. God is not an isolationist. He does not separate people the way man does. When someone disagrees with us, we value him less, sideline him, discount him as not having a contribution to anything because he does not agree with us. But the ambassadors of the King think differently. They see humanity. They have become "species aware." That is, some understand they cannot destroy their own kind.

If a species is to survive, there must mutual respect, mutual care, and responsibility. Nature itself teaches us this. The instincts of the animal kingdoms know as much, yet we, as human beings, seem to have lost that awareness, that sense of mutual contribution and need.

A pride of lions lives in harmony. They do not kill one another, abuse one another's young. Science says we are descendants of apes, yet apes treat each other with more honor than human beings do.

The King did not create man for a religious purpose or a political purpose. He created us to add value to creation. The intention of the King is to see all humanity loved, gathered, protected, empowered, and contributing to the well-being of His creation. But man duped himself into gathering to like-minded groupings. Whether religious, political, or cultural, man builds walls around his beliefs and condemns all those who do not see life from his vantage point. He has no species awareness, no matter how humanitarian he may sound. There is no hope, no redemption, no prosperity in that way of thinking. When the King is allowed to set up His Life within, there is a transformational union between the King and man. We now call him the God-man. He is neither under the slavery of his instinctive animal nature nor is he condescending to those of a religious belief system. Something very powerful happens. Something otherworldly blossoms within man. He no longer lives for himself, but he lives for the well-being of all men. He does not condemn; he saves. He does not build walls of separation; he gathers. He does not silence or discredit the opposing voice; he listens. He may disagree, but he loves and empowers them. He allows the King to live and love through him. The attributes, power, and purposes of the King's Life are of paramount importance to these God-men, and to that end they live and to that end they sometimes die.

The ambassadors of the King see humanity in a whole new light in that everyone has an invaluable contribution to the rest of humanity. Every life is important; no, every life is critical to the advancement of humanity's well-being and the well-being of all creation.

The King knows that everyone has an invaluable contribution to the rest of us. He created everyone with gifts and abilities. When some are marginalized, the world suffers for lack of their contribution. The lack that we see in the world is due to many not having the opportunity to step into their destiny. When human rights are violated, the contribution to the world is absent. The absence of their individual gift in the earth makes us all lesser people and makes our world less than the King has intended.

What would the world be like if all were able to fulfill their God-given destiny? How would we be living right now if each person fulfilled the dream the King had for them? What would we be talking about right now? What would be lacking? What would be missing? The question is not what would we have achieved but rather what would be the human condition if everyone would have been able to bring their contribution to the world?

When the King walked the earth, He never spoke to death but only to potential. The God-Man speaks to potential. He speaks to the often dormant potential within each person. Like their King, these God-men speak Life, wholeness, strength, and power. Their very words release the possibilities within and empower them to fruition. With no regard to their own achievements, they are thrilled to see those around them become all the King had in mind for them.

When I (Dr. Don) was speaking in Pescara, Italy, there was a retired pastor attending my talks. After one talk, this man approached me with tears in his eyes and, through a translator, asked me if God still had a destiny for him. As I looked at him, I could feel the love of the King well up within me. I sensed that the King had something special to say to this veteran soldier of the King. "As long as you breathe," I began, "the King's Life flows from you and destiny always unfolds before you." This 93-year-old preacher in Italy is like most of us—he needed to know that his life was important, he was needed, his life meant something.

We all benefit when each person is free to make his contribution to the world. A person's value is not measured by his religion, his education, his family, or his economic status. Destiny is color blind, culturally unaware, never mindful of religious, political, financial, or geographic considerations. The seeds of human possibilities bloom in whatever condition they find themselves. They should not be marginalized or dominated by smaller minds and restrictive environments. The truly spiritual of the earth will not allow religious prejudice to disrupt the plans of the King in the hungry heart. The contribution within each person is intended to change the human condition for the better, breaking the barriers that attempt to keep destiny in check. For destiny will always interfere with mediocrity. It will always challenge the status quo. By its very existence, destiny rebukes the naysayer, resists the proud, and redefines what it means to be human. It will always break the status quo so that the wonders of creation can be experienced and the fullest potential of humanity can be discovered. The hope of the world is that those who claim allegiance to the King will see the intrinsic value of all men and work to make room for every man's contribution to the good of all creation.

Peacemakers at Heart

The ambassador of the Kingdom is, by his new nature, a peacemaker. He is at peace with himself because he is at peace with God. He is at peace with all men because the peace of the King has found a home within him. The peace of the King permeates the life of the citizen in every area of life. His peace forms our beliefs, adjusts our politics, and paints a picture of humanity that few have seen. For His peace is toward all men. He does not love the Christian more than the atheist or the Muslim. He does not endorse war to establish peace or put a higher value on one nation over another. We are all His and all have the honor of being loved by Him. There is no room for hyper-politicization in His Kingdom. The kingdoms of this world are destined to become the domain of the King. But He does it in love, patience, compassion, forgiveness. His peace should literally fill the room when you enter and be the source of confident hope to all you come in contact with.

Once again, His Kingdom, because it comes from within, cannot be legislated from the top. It is always a force that is sourced from within where the King is already establishing His Kingdom. As a man is in his heart, so he cannot help to be in life. Either there is genuine inner transformation or we are just another person hawking our wares like everyone else. What should make us stand apart is not our marketing program, not even out talent. What truly sets us apart is the King and His inner governance within our hearts. If folks don't see it, no amount of glitter can imitate His glory, no amount of talk will bring hope, and no amount of guilt can make folks see what is clearly not just within. The Peace of the King is confident, encouraging, hopeful, loving, forgiving, and solid as the Rock.

The King has established the constitution and by-laws for His Kingdom. These words are the very heart of the inner rule of the King. They are the fruit-proof evidence that the King is reigning within the heart. For this constitution is the autobiography of Him-self, His nature, His passion, and the love of His Father in whom the

King lives. When you read these words, understand that your King is describing His Life. When you see these attributes flowing from you, it is a good indication that His governance is taking hold within. On the other hand, when some of these are absent, we realize that we have yet to surrender that part of our lives to Him. We live "in part" because we surrender "in part." Therefore, the part of ourselves we surrender will be the part that expresses the Life of the King. The frustration comes when we see the duality of the King nature and human nature coexisting in the same body. A life of Broken repentance is our best opportunity to live in the King and the King in us.

> *If I speak with the tongues of men and of angels, but do not have love, I have become a noisy gong or a clanging cymbal. If I have the gift of prophecy, and know all mysteries and all knowledge; and if I have all faith, so as to remove mountains, but do not have love, I am nothing. And if I give all my possessions to feed the poor, and if I surrender my body to be burned, but do not have love, it profits me nothing* (1 Corinthians 13:1–3).

Just as we are encouraged to focus on love rather than the individual gifts we might possess, so too, focusing on love sets us up for the surrender of our entire being. It allows the process of brokenness to make us aware instantly of our human responses, which generally do not end well in difficult situations. We no longer live a half-surrendered life, but we have yielded ourselves as far as we can see. But that does not excuse us; quite to the contrary, we walk more softly, more circumspectly. We come to realize that a quick answer is not as important as a loving response; winning an argument is not as important as winning our opponent as a friend. That does not mean we give in to their perspective, but it means our response in love and humility will go much further than trying to slaughter your opponent with facts—all in the Name of the King, of course.

As you might have guessed by now, it is all about the King and His ways—Kingdom rule within the human heart. The words of the King's constitution will become more than words as He gently writes them upon your heart. For when He writes His ways on your heart, you have changed; you have brought your relationship with the King beyond mere words. Now you have become one with Him and His ways are now the passionate desire of your heart.

Blessed are the poor in spirit, for theirs is the kingdom of heaven. Blessed are those who mourn, for they shall be comforted. Blessed are the gentle, for they shall inherit the earth. Blessed are those who hunger and thirst for righteousness, for they shall be satisfied. Blessed are the merciful, for they shall receive mercy. Blessed are the pure in heart, for they shall see God. Blessed are the peacemakers, for they shall be called sons of God. Blessed are those who have been persecuted for the sake of righteousness, for theirs is the kingdom of heaven. Blessed are you when people insult you and persecute you, and falsely say all kinds of evil against you because of Me. Rejoice and be glad, for your reward in heaven is great; for in the same way they persecuted the prophets who were before you (Matthew 5:3–12).

CHAPTER FIVE

Inner Governance: The Power of the Forgotten Mountain

I have done my best over the years to live my life according to what I have been taught. I wanted more than anything, and still want more than anything, for my life to reflect the love of God to all I meet. Whether or not I deem a person worthy of that love is immaterial as my prejudices have tainted my decisions and spoiled my attempts at Divine expression more than once. This very personal frustration with the actions over which I seemed to have no control lead me to imposing upon myself stricter rules of thought and attitude. I have forced myself to bury the deep-rooted patterns of belief that I have always battled. Unfortunately, it did not work. I found myself loving those most easily loved and then congratulating myself on such open-mindedness. I gathered those easiest to gather, prayed for those easiest to pray for. I gave to those whom I knew would someday be able to help me. I developed my beliefs according to what others had taught me was correct and refrained from feelings that would demonstrate a lack of love, tolerance, inclusion only to find myself in denial when these feelings surfaced and then boiling with inner turmoil and anger that they were still alive and well within, in spite of my best efforts.

I came to the conclusion, quite reluctantly, that I could not be like Jesus, no matter how hard I tried. I looked around me and saw many believers apparently living in a much greater level of victory than I. How were they living such a submitted life? How were they able to give so freely of themselves to all those around them? It was truly a conundrum of the highest level. I concluded that either these folks were living in the same denial as I was living in or they had discovered an answer that had so far eluded me. As much as I hated to admit it, it was clear that the issues of the heart cannot be legislated. Yet unless the heart is either legislated or somehow changed, there is no permanent change in me or in society. I was desperate for both, but I was smart enough to understand that it had to begin with me. I must personally become the change I wanted to see in the world around me. It was a cliché, but it was a truthful cliché! But change was apparently impossible in myself.

I am now on this journey for many years, and I tell you with certainty that, try as I might, as hard as I might, a change of heart is elusive at best and temporary when it is achieved. Am I the only one who has struggled with this? I had to be honest with myself. Personal inner governance was a losing battle. My choices were as few as they were unacceptable. I could accept the inevitability of my ungovernable heart and do my best to suppress the feelings I hated. I could also just go with the feelings as they were and develop doctrines that permitted these feelings. I could also live in seclusion and thus avoid contact with those who stirred these feeling up. But none of these would fulfill my most earnest desire—to be authentic in my faith and in my presentation of that faith to the world. I would need inner governance on a scale that I did not know existed.

I reasoned that there was only one way to permanently see the nature and character of the King in my life. I would have to relinquish personal control of my life to Him. But I had tried that. I had prayed again and again to submit to Him. I rebuked my attitudes, renounced, denounced, decreed, and I even tried to fast them away, but to no avail. It was then I made a most stunning discovery, one that would truly change my life's course. I would have to die. Of course not physically, but I would have to truly give everything I hated about what I could not control to the King. I would have to die to myself so He could live His own life through me. There is the authentic life of the believer. There is the authentic display of the Life of the King through mere mortal man. The King would be free to live, not just in me but through me.

The Established Plumb Line

The Mountain of the Lord, the place where true Divine authority is first established, is established in the hearts of men and women. When His Life is the ruling authority within, that same ruling authority rules everything that is touched. Make no mistake, this Life cannot be imitated, nor can it be turned into a systematic policy that attempts change from the top down, from the outside in. The governance of the King is within. The rule of the King is first in the individual heart and only then does it radiate to the world, beginning with those around you. The evidence of genuine Divine inner governance is clear, for it is the central focus of Jesus as He lives out His Life today through those who will allow Him such unprecedented access to their heart. The only valid evidence of His inner governance is the presence of the fruit of this Divine Life: love, joy, peace, patience, gentleness, goodness, meekness, self-control, and faith. God made a way for these Divine attributes to come naturally, abide permanently, and shine wholeheartedly. It is certainly clear that one cannot rule righteously if he is not himself ruled by righteousness. The fruit-proof of the King's reign within the heart is, without question, His Life, visible and flowing in all we are, all we say, all we do. The safeguard of this governance is the predictable presence of joy, wholeness, hope, peace, love. It is no wonder then that this Divine inner reality cannot be faked. If the love of Christ controls us, we are under His governance. If we are under His governance, then His nature has taken root within and He is seen clearly in our lives.

For the love of Christ controls us, having concluded this, that one died for all, therefore all died; and He died for all, so that they who live might no longer live for themselves, but for Him who died and rose again on their behalf (2 Corinthians 5:14-15).

Eternal Disconnect

For centuries, believers have always thought that their faith was something that would bring untold, unmeasurable blessing to their lives—and it does. They always thought that the King was there to take care of their every need—and He does. But the primary discovery of my life was in discovering that I lived not for my own satisfaction and fulfillment of my plans, but for the will of the King. The key to a life of fulfillment and peace was not in getting everything I want but in doing everything the King wants of me. Therefore, I must change. There would be no more disconnect between my faith and everyday life. What I truly believed would result in how I lived every day. The most difficult admission was that if I did not live it, then I did not really, really believe it. Faith without works was truly dead. For faith changes the heart which, in turn, changes how I live. There needed to be a change of inner governance. Simply put, I had to die to myself that He might live.

The Big Question

If there is no inner governance of the King, one's personal life cannot be governed effectively, joyfully, lovingly, compassionately. If the King does not govern the heart, nothing will be effectively governed.

Ever since God gave Moses the Ten Commandments, governments have passed thousands of laws attempting to control the actions of men. Like Mount Sinai, laws written in rocks or on paper will never bring change within. The human heart, unchecked as it is, always finds a way around laws or it simply ignores them. Man will do whatever he wants given enough time to figure his way around the imposed restrictions of society and government. On the other hand, Mount Zion, the Mountain of the House of the Lord, writes the laws of our Lord on our hearts. He supernaturally changes us to *desire* His inner governance.

As stated earlier, God gave us the Ten Commandments to show us how we cannot keep to a civilized, moral standard of living. For the law does not eradicate; rather, it exposes the rebellious, wanton passions of man. If we have learned anything over the time man has been on this planet, it is that without a heart change, actions will never permanently change. The Age of Enlightenment, the Age of Aquarius, the New Age Movement, the Renaissance, even the Arab Spring did not bring the kind of change that some thought had arrived.

Human emotions are fickle, even deceiving. We often think we have made life-changing discoveries only to realize much later that we were deceived by our own emotional response to a situation. Something that seemed so real was later found to be nothing at all. That is the issue. An emotionally driven desire will eventually fade. One cannot maintain an attitude of peace and harmony in his own strength indefinitely. The heart must change if true inner governance is to be maintained.

The King is the only One who changes the heart. He is the constant, the steadiness, the trustworthy inner force that both writes His immutable love on our hearts and then teaches us to lovingly respond to that love. He shows us the way, changes our heart, and then gives us the power and the favor to do it. A changed heart is the only way to *be* the peace we want to see in the earth. A heart controlled by Him brings about His will in the earth. His governance within and without, as evidenced by the fruit of His Spirit, establishes lasting fulfillment for us individually and internationally. These words are easier to write than they are to follow, and I do not write them in a vacuum.

I have come face to face with my own weaknesses, my own failures, my own inability to follow my own path that I so nobly declared and personally embraced. I come to the place of realization that I, too—I especially—need the King. I need the King to rule first in my heart and then display His Kingly reign to the world. My heart must be governable by the King. The question must be asked by all men. Who is reigning in your heart? Most of us believe that God is reigning within. But we miss the bigger picture because our personal desires and agenda cloud the work of God within. We have *learned* what to do without *becoming*. So we have not learned as we should, therefore we cannot *become*, because becoming only comes through dying. The Kingdom is where the King reigns. It is not a building, a government, or a religious denomination. It is within. "I have been crucified with Christ; and it is no longer I who live, but Christ lives in me; and the life which I now live in the flesh I live by faith in the Son of God, who loved me and gave Himself up for me" (Gal. 2:20).

Our Limit

How can He live through me if I am still alive? Only one can rule. When there is more than one life, there is a mixture. Our lives are constantly being challenged by the love and power of the One Life within. The King is about His Father's business. He is at work in the lives of all men to bring them to the place of true inner governance of the King. But this is not an easy thing to accomplish. No wonder the Scripture compares this to death. We instinctively fight death no matter how it appears to threaten us. We humans are a stubborn and proud lot. We do not easily change. We do not easily die, do not admit that another is right.

Unfortunately, we all have our limits. Change will be easily accepted when that change is certain to benefit us in some way. But what happens when that change means we must surrender even our most sacred beliefs? This is where we begin to struggle, argue, even search the Scripture for some kind of spiritual resolution that proves what we already believe. But take special note of that day, that point of resistance, for it makes the end of your death. The end of your change. Resistance is not futile. In fact, resistance is the end of the line for our own ongoing effectiveness.

One of the most difficult things I have ever heard the Lord speak to my heart was when He said that His Life must trump everything, even politics. I will say it again, plainly. The Kingdom within must trump politics. It is true, most folks will change their religion before they will change their politics. Deep within, we truly believe more strongly in the power of political ideology than we do anything else. But even our deepest held political beliefs must come under the scrutiny of Christ's inner governance. Now, I can almost hear some thinking as they read this that they know folks who need to hear this. Some are thinking that I am affirming their politics by writing this. Quite to the contrary, if any of those aforementioned thoughts ran through your mind, it is evidence that your politicking days, at least the way you have believed, are over. Many will call me unpatriotic to say this. I am not afraid of that happening. I have discovered that as much as I love this country and so appreciate her freedoms and possibilities to anyone who will work for them, my citizenship is of another country. I look to Him first, foremost, and absolutely. The laws of mere mortals and the governments they create ultimately turn on the average folks to maintain their own power and control. It is true in politics, religion, business, and culture. Spiritually ungoverned man will, in the last analysis, do what is best for himself.

It has been a hard and difficult journey of discovery. I am a citizen of the Kingdom of God and rule of the King is consuming my heart and life. I want it to be no other way. My ways are not His; my will is not His; my opinions are not His; my politics are not His. I no longer expect any human government to rule compassionately on behalf of the people. I refuse to look to human government, no matter what form or party or strong man is in charge. Until we look unwaveringly to the King for governance, both inner and outer, we are missing the mark by a country mile.

All the Mountains

Most everyone wants to be a king or they want to be *the* King. We are driven by the inner need to feel important, needed, loved.

Unfortunately, we think that rulership comes with heavy-handedness, intimidation, indoctrination, ruthless efforts to keep the folks in line. But even a cursory look at history shows that this kind of governance does not work for very long, and where it does work, even for a short time, the people are under a heavy burden of fear, sorrow, and uncertainty. The King rules from a heart of love, honor, compassion, and peace. His goal is the well-being of all men. But He is also "hard wired" to a process that is equally righteous.

Some will teach that the end result, if it is good, justifies any means of getting there. But there can be no righteous end where an unrighteous means of getting there is acceptable. For that unrighteous means makes the end result unrighteous, so matter how holy the original intent. For evil methods taint the heart and skew the message, the messenger, and the mission. Do not be deceived. If the King is leading, He will lead to a righteous end with righteous methods and wholesome results. Everyone inevitably wins when the rule of the Righteous One governs from His throne within the heart.

All the other mountains of authority are governed from what is in a man's heart. Man is the ultimate authority over all things natural. When man submits his mandated dominance over the earth to the King, man can truly rule anything effectively. If one wants to change either the mountain he rules or the mountain that rules him, he must change the heart, his own heart. If one wants to change his heart, he must submit to the rule of the King on the Mountain of His House within. The heart that can be governed by the King can govern anything; it can even govern a nation.

I am not discouraged by the apparent void of His inner governance in the hearts of men. For I am more than convinced that if He can reach me then He can reach anyone. I have a tendency to view the world from my own point of view. I see myself as one person among the teeming billions of people and wonder how things could ever change. Nonetheless, there is another view—His view. He is at work in countless people just as He is at work in you and me, and He is bringing His plan to fruition through folks we do not know living in countries whose names we may not be able to pronounce. This is my confidence and this is my personal assurance. He who has begun a good work in me will bring it to its fullness in His time. My responsibility is to care for all that is in my sphere of influence, my circle of relationship, and trust Him for the rest. When I can completely give myself to Him for His work within, I am winning.

> *For a child will be born to us* [me], *a son will be given to us* [me]; *and the government will rest on His shoulders* [authority of man]; *and His name will be called Wonderful Counselor, Mighty God, Eternal Father, Prince of Peace. There will be no end to the increase of His government or of peace* [in us], *on the throne of David and over his kingdom, to establish it and to uphold it with justice and righteousness from then on and forevermore* (Isaiah 9:6-7).

Isaiah saw something so powerful when he saw the King's governance on the shoulders of the King within. He saw what few have seen thus far. He saw the increase of peace, fatherhood, and stability. He saw the Kingdom and the King in the proper alignment on earth because it was in proper alignment with people. Governments do not heal the land, people do.

Jesus taught us a prayer that is repeated millions of times each week, yet few understand its impact as God answers the prayer among men.

> *Pray, then, in this way: "Our Father who is in heaven, hallowed be Your name.*
> *Your kingdom come.*
> *Your will be done, on earth as it is in heaven"* (Matthew 6:9-10).

Jesus taught us to pray for His Kingdom to come to earth, for His will to be done among men as it is done in heaven. He cried out, "Repent, for the Kingdom of God is at hand!"

The Man Becomes the Message

To that extent, the personal lifestyle of the individual is critical. One cannot represent a spiritual Kingdom and its King when there is dichotomy in the heart. The man, the message, the principles of His Kingdom are both all natural and all spiritual. The man, then, becomes the message. The union of the heart of man and the heart of the King produces a fragrance that is otherworldly yet very much observable in time and space. What exists as theory to the intellectual becomes the reality of this union between he who was a mere man and his God. Everything God is becomes planted in the broken, repentant heart. At this point, everything changes. Everything becomes both natural and spiritual as the thoughts of man are now the thoughts of God and the thoughts of God are now the thoughts of man. They become indistinguishable as the rule of Kingdom love blurs the lines between man and God. The Word spoken becomes the Word expressed, but not merely expressed; it is actually materialized in this dimension through those who have surrendered to His inner governance. Communication with the King is no longer an external experience of dreams, visions, angels, prophetic impartations, and serendipitous events. Now the communication between the King and His people becomes indistinguishable thoughts, emotions, and feelings as the King influences, changes the mind and heart of the priest of the Presence. It is this Word within that discerns the heart of God from opinions, doctrines, and politics—even religious politics of mere mortal man.

This is not a matter of outward conformation but of inner surrender to the One who lives within, thus proving the validity, the literal reality of His Divine Kingdom governance within. For this Kingly governance within reaches the deepest parts of our being where Christ has established His throne. All that He is flows from the place of inward governance and surrender.

The King is Coming…in You

Many believers look to see the King coming on a cloud at the end of the age. They believe there is little or nothing for them to do in the meantime. I am not here to simply debate a religious eschatology; rather, my goal is to present the passion of the King for the lives of all men and women whoever they are and wherever they live. There is an appearing of which I am certain and in which I am an active participant. The King will appear in people all over the earth before He is ever seen breaking through the clouds in the sky. Yes, the King is coming. He is coming in you. The responsibility is yours, the calling is yours, and the destiny is most definitely yours. No matter what specific calling you have in your life to fulfill, you are destined to fulfill it to the max under the governance of the King.

This inner governance, this Kingdom expression of the King Himself and all He represents flows outward from a heart that is truly ruled by the King who dwells within. Inner governance is the evidence of true yieldedness to the Life of the King. When the King rules the heart, we can be assured that the intentions of the King are followed. They are not tainted by the personal ambitions of man. The fruit in the life of His ambassadors as well as the principles of this Kingdom are plainly visible to all, and there is truly peace and harmonious growth among men.

This Divine passion is rising in the earth. It is expressed through those who yield to His inner governance. It is a noble passion, a powerful determination that responds to the needs of the earth and her inhabitants. This passion does not pre-judge, does not discriminate, is not beholden to anyone, and is committed to restore creativity and innovation to the human spirit through the direction and governance of the King. It is ushering in a new age of spiritual fulfillment. They see through politically and religiously correct ideologies and instead are ushering in a time of selflessness and true honor, compassion, understanding, love, and love's corresponding actions.

These folks are out of the control of man, but they are coming under the control of a compassionate and loving God through Whom the answers flow to a desperate world. These folks have discovered the Mountain of the House of the Lord is within. They have committed themselves to fall into the ranks of the committed Redeemed. They have discovered their Redeemer lives to restore mankind body, soul, and spirit. Their words match their actions; their attitudes match the loving God Who indwells them. Their hearts overflow with a love that overcomes all obstacles, all arguments, and all fear. For these will love where hate once ruled. They will heal where disease and war have poisoned the earth. They will gather where separation, religion, ethnic cleansing, and racism have dominated.

> *For the love of Christ controls us, having concluded this, that one died for all, therefore all died; and He died for all, so that they who live might no longer live for themselves, but for Him who died and rose again on their behalf* (2 Corinthians 5:14-15).

What Happens When the Heart Changes?

When the heart changes, everything changes, for from the heart flow the issues of life. From the heart all our decisions are made, beliefs are determined, and love is born. From the heart purpose is ignited, and from the heart destiny is seen and embraced. A changed heart will change the mind, change priorities, passions, and plans. A changed heart causes joy to leap and hope to abound. A changed heart loves freely, forgives quickly, and gathers wholeheartedly. A changed heart is unwavering, faithful, reliable, and consistent. It is compassionate and loving, encouraging and confident.

Yes, a changed heart changes everything. It is as transformational as it is exciting, trustworthy as it is determined. A changed heart has surrendered to the King. Now His rule and reign begin to flow from the life of the changed heart and the whole world benefits.

When the heart is changed, the Word has become flesh within; the King begins His righteous reign; His Kingdom is established within. This change is so profound that this very private inner governance can be easily seen from without. For this heart change, this inner governance cannot be contained but broadcasts its eternal and healing light for all to see and experience.

And the Word became flesh, and dwelt among us, and we saw His glory, glory as of the only begotten from the Father, full of grace and truth (John 1:14).

If the word does not become flesh, there is no visible demonstration of genuine Kingdom rule in the heart. Only a changed heart can sustain inner governance and this inner governance is the only authentic evidence that the Word indeed is becoming flesh.

How Does Transformation Happen?

Authentic transformation is the supernatural activity of the King in the heart of an individual. The heart changes, is transformed when there is clear, absolute surrender in an area of one's life. This surrender, also called repentance, releases the power and purposes of God to replace the surrendered area with the Life of Christ, the King of the Mountain of the Lord. As Paul the apostle confessed, "I die daily" (1 Cor. 15:31). Death to the earthy side of us releases the spiritual force of God to gain access to our mind, thus changing it to represent the new thing that is now happening within our hearts. The more sincere the surrender, the more radical the takeover of the King within. No wonder those who are forgiven rejoice much. Surrender releases the burden of regret, shame, guilt, and inner torment that reigns when our fleshy self controls our lives. There is no doubt that the rule of the King produces peace where there was once only the pain of failure. Jesus, of course, said it best, "Come to Me, all who are weary and heavy-laden, and I will give you rest. Take My yoke upon you and learn from Me, for I am gentle and humble in heart, and you will find rest for your souls. For My yoke is easy and My burden is light" (Matt. 11:28–30).

Once a person has experienced the liberating freedom of forgiveness, empowerment, and hope of the King, it often sets a course of life that enhances the rule of the King. The new path is a daily mission of personal sacrifice, knowing that to be transformed from mere mortals to those embodying themselves with the King is their best hope for continuous fulfillment personally, publicly, and spiritually.

The process of this inner transformation is lifelong. A new way of thinking is overtaking the heart, and a new determination has settled in the soul. Now they will see everyone differently.

> *Therefore from now on we recognize no one according to the flesh; even though we have known Christ according to the flesh, yet now we know Him in this way no longer. Therefore if anyone is in Christ, he is a new creature; the old things passed away; behold, new things have come* (2 Corinthians 5:16-17).

The decision to make this radical change in thinking does not come overnight, nor is it a one-time event. Rather, it is lifelong commitment to the rule of the King and His governance within the heart.

Neither a religious experience nor a secular assignment, this inner governance is responsible for the formation of Christ the King within the heart. For the words of one's mouth cannot be divorced from that person's actions. They are one and the same. It is the commitment to this inner formation of the King that gives hope to the possibility that peace can rule in the hearts of men and that peace can absolutely bring about global brotherhood and mutual care. There truly is no other way.

The evidence of the formation of the King within is undeniable:

> *So every good tree bears good fruit, but the bad tree bears bad fruit. A good tree cannot produce bad fruit, nor can a bad tree produce good fruit. Every tree that does not bear good fruit is cut down and thrown into the fire. So then, you will know them by their fruits. Not everyone who says to Me, "Lord, Lord" will enter the kingdom of heaven, but he who does the will of My Father who is in heaven will enter* (Matthew 7:17–21).

A remarkable thing happens to those committed to this new and emerging inner formation. They are becoming the message of the King in their actions, their attitudes, and their outlook. Replacing the heart of a mere mortal is an act of the King Himself, who now begins to live, to flourish, to shine from those who are giving themselves to the King.

With the evidence of transformation so specific, it cannot be faked. Words will no longer win the masses. They have been wronged so many times before. There is no wiggle room in this inner governance. The position of ambassador emerges as the heart changes. It is as inevitable as it is revolutionary. This ambassadorship is not proven by an official document. It is proven by the consistency and authenticity of a person's actions. Fruit is the proof of everything authentic. Just as Jesus told the Jews of the first century, "If you are Abraham's children, do the deeds of Abraham" (John 8:39), so the plumb line is in Him. It follows, then, that the same plumb line is within, either proving or disproving the confession of our mouth and actions of our heart.

Those demonstrated actions are clearly described as the ones that prove not only citizenship of the Mountain of the Lord but the role as an ambassador. "But the fruit of the Spirit is love, joy, peace, longsuffering, gentleness, goodness, faith, meekness, temperance…. And they that are Christ's have crucified the flesh with the affections and lusts. If we live in the Spirit, let us also walk in the Spirit" (Gal. 5:22–25 KJV).

This is such a simple, hopeful, engaging, and empowering passage. The ways of mere mortal, self-centered, power hungry, self-indulgent humanity give way to the love-driven, Life-giving, mercy- and compassion-filled ambassadors who are themselves filled with the Life of the King who rules within them. These have authenticity in the inner man. You can trust them. They are predictable, approachable, understanding, and compassionate to a fault. They confess their mistakes and resist their weaknesses knowing that personal weakness left ungoverned is a profoundly negative reflection on the King and the Kingdom they represent. Paul was overwhelmed with the responsibility he carried as he said, "I am the least of the apostles, and not fit to be called an apostle" (1 Cor. 15:9). When some tried to worship him as a god, he ripped at his clothing a cried out, "I am a man just like you!" (see Acts 14:15). He knew himself apart from the inner governance of the King and was unwilling to give it even a tiny excuse to dominate his life. To Paul, really to all those who carry the Presence of the King within, disparaging actions which inevitably bring into question the validity of the King's rule are an anathema to them. The very thought of such a thing is appalling to them.

Paul understood like very few understood then and even fewer understand now. We must be transformed. The salvation of the Lord Jesus results in many awesome things. But primarily, salvation will *transform* us from the inside out. If there is nothing that is transformed, salvation is not at work. Jesus's resurrection is much more than a ticket to heaven and entrance into a "bless me" club. The apostle's focus was so clear, so simple, so determined. He was redeemed that he might be transformed.

The transformed life is the clearest sermon one can preach. It is the most compelling evidence, the most powerful proof that Divine inner governance is not only possible, it is happening. It is the eternal song that fills the heart with joy and the world with hope. Paul's heart passion was to be daily, continuously transformed by the power and love of God. He wanted the world to know that Christ lived in and through him. He wanted to be transformed. So do I.

The Education of Discomfort

Discomfort is not a sign of the enemy. We rebuke the enemy when something is happening we do not like. We resist what we do not agree with. We rebuke, condemn, and discredit anyone who sees things differently or causes pain. Jesus learned obedience through the things He suffered, but we just want to cover ourselves with our belief and ignore the circumstances we are in. Most have us have learned long ago how to kill the messenger. But many times, the messenger is the King. The more we resist, the tougher the messenger has to be to deliver the Words of the King.

Difficult circumstances, if we allow them, will show us where we need to surrender, where we need to die. It is a blessed condition indeed. Growth does not come from mere study of anything, even the Bible. Growth is the result of surrender to whatever it is we have studied and have determined is more critical to our desired lifestyle and destiny. We do it subconsciously in many cases. But for the more foundational changes, conscious, sober consideration precedes a decision to surrender and ultimately change. To be sure, without the difficulties that often stun us with our apparent inability to cope, change is intellectual, religious, or at least so shallow that we can be easily convinced to another direction or cause. Changes brought about by trials stick to our being more than we have realized in the past.

True maturity is understanding that every difficult circumstance, every provocative person, every bump in the road is an opportunity to hear from the King. Even if one does not accept that everything is from the King, everything can be turned to good when we have the resolve to go to the King rather than to our arsenal of spiritual, emotional weapons to deliver us from the thing we do not like.

Christ-yielded lives have surrendered, died, relinquished themselves, their pride, and their intellect to Him who really does have the answers, the plan, the love and power to bring about the kind of harmony and peace the world craves. Man has never needed to try to figure things out in himself; he has only needed to die to himself so that King could live freely through him. Even though death is not fun, is not comfortable, it is this surrender that makes way for the King on the earth. This is truly the hope of the world. The King in me, the King in you is the hope of the glory that He has intended to cover the earth as the water covers the seas. The Christ-yielded life is the spiritual formation that brings permanent change. The Christ-centered life is religion's attempt to keep order with external programs, protocols, and policies.

The Genuine Life

If the truth be really told, this thing we call inner governance by the King cannot be faked. It does not matter the eloquence of the words spoken, the number of Bible verses quoted, the size or number of the organizations one has started, or the titles one carries. The absolute reality of the King's Presence cannot be faked. No, you cannot fake this emerging of His mighty love as He arises within His people. He is sovereign. He is engaging. He is consuming. His Presence shuts the mouth of His detractors. Get ready—He is coming…in you, then through you. The King of a Kingdom not of this world is appearing in all His regal glory in the lives of those who have done more than merely mouthed the words of true Lordship, but have given themselves to the death of their own ways in order to be heralds of a Life, a power, a love, a Kingdom that is not of this world but should be evident in the world; not of this dimension but should be flourishing in it; not of this humanity but has always been intended to be thriving within our hearts.

This needs to be very clear. This inner governance, this Kingdom expression of the King is not a matter of outward conformation but of inner surrender to the One who lives within. His reality within proves the validity, the literal existence of His Kingdom and the power that raised Him from the dead to reign as King of this Kingdom for ever and ever. This inner governance reaches the deepest parts of our being where the King has established His throne. From this inward place of His dwelling within flows His Life-consciousness, His love, His forgiveness, His authority, and His passion for a redeemed, delivered, and healed humanity. Only when His Kingdom is securely planted within will its outworking affect the world.

Why should it be any different? The King of this Kingdom is a benevolent lover all things right, all things whole and peaceful. His rule would flow from the hearts of those who have most certainly died to the ways of unregenerated humanity. His sovereign rule gathers, heals, loves, nourishes, and creates an environment of hope that reaches all men and trickles into all the dark corners of human existence. It shines its eternal light on what is wrong and recreates those things into everything that grows so that peace prevails and hope empowers even the least of us to accomplish mighty things.

This is not an old man's dream, it is the reality of the Divine doing His mighty work through those who have been arrested by His love and changed by beholding Him within. I have seen folks transformed by Him before my eyes. Ha! I have watched myself change before my eyes! I had never realized what could happen when a person relinquished control of his life, his will to Jesus. Then it began to happen to me. I still see it every day. I watched fear, real fear, fear of everything fall to the ground in a moment of time. I watched my desires change, my passions change. I saw despair, so deeply lodged within my heart, disappear in a moment of time. My mind began to change so quickly that I was dizzy with joy, with the anticipation at what was happening within me, quite out of my own control.

The sobering flip side is that not everything dies so easily. It is one thing to repent of the actions you hate. It is another thing entirely to repent of the things you love, even though you know they are wrong. Ancient Israel wanted to leave the slavery of the Egypt they hated, but they resisted crossing the Jordan River. They would have to leave the sin they craved in the wilderness. But even that is a good fight. For there is where brokenness humbles me to leave my own private wilderness so that the things surrendered to the King die once and for all. Brokenness constantly reminds me of my weakness so I will ever cling to His love and His power within my own life. If I cannot allow His power to reign within, how can I ever expect Him to allow me to rule anything else?

> *He who is slow to anger is better than the mighty, and he who rules his spirit, than he who captures a city* (Proverbs 16:32).

Destined to Live

To be sure, there would be times when I would try to wrestle that control back from Him, humanity being what it is. But there was one thing of which I was certain. I was destined to die. Therefore, I was also destined to live, to be raised up in a new Life of peace, courage, love, compassion, and humility every day. No wonder Jeremiah said

His mercies are new every morning (see Lam. 3:23). I was destined to give up my own everything to take up His everything. It was true! In the light of His Life within I could clearly see that my everything was grossly overrated and embarrassingly insufficient to do what the King Himself had ordained for my Life. Only His everything would have the power, the wisdom, and most of all the love to do what He had dreamed for me. His everything was far from the traditional platitudes, expectations, and duties of a merely religious person.

No, this was not religion; this was and is reality. This is truly the King, living, moving, and having His way, His *everything* in the likes of a simple, broken human being like me. His sovereign rule gathers, heals, loves, nourishes, and creates an environment of hope that trickles into all the dark corners of human existence. It shines its eternal light on what is wrong and recreates those things into everything that grows so that peace prevails and hope empowers even the least, the last of us to accomplish mighty things according to the dreams He has already dreamed for us. This is God's everything transforming this clay pot into something that would be a Lamp of His Anointed Son. No one could have planned this. No one could have taught this, for it is accomplished in the Secret Place of His Presence in the deepest part of our hearts. This is where true transformation occurs. This is the Kingdom within.

This, then, is the priesthood and the kingship that He has ordained for every believer. It is the destiny He had written on our hearts long before He formed us in the depths of our mother's womb. This is the role of the ambassadors sent by the King the world craves—those who are the reality of the King who indwells them. Those who die moment by moment see Him live His majestic Life moment by moment through mere humanity turned mighty because of the King.

CHAPTER SIX

Ambassador Kings

The King is gathering willing men and women who stand in the Presence of the King to be transformed into His likeness and image. Once this transformation begins, there is another, very different role that these priests will fulfill. As they are priests before God, they are kings before man.

The Priests of Melchizedek are Godward; that is, they are intensely God-focused. They are in the process of inner transformation that will make them ambassadors of the King Himself. But they are not just ministers to God as priests. They also minister to the world as ambassador-kings. They yield to the King so that His Divine Nature is securely founded within as well as evident by the Kingly fruit of their governance. In short, they are real to the bone. These are folks who have been bought by the atoning blood of Jesus Christ and have been refined in the crucible of affliction. They are friends to Brokenness and they have made their covenant with Him by sacrifice. They live in broken repentance and are yielding daily to the will of the One who has sent them, so they are always open to instruction, correction, rebuke, and direction. They have learned the voice of the King and have His laws written on their hearts. Their goal—inner transformation so the inner governance of the King becomes a way of life for them.

The King has made these ambassadors both kings and priests. They not only understand the role of the King and the Priest but they embody both in their own life. Both positions abide within the lives of ambassadors. Although both functions affect the whole man, they can be distinctly evident according to where the King sends them. To the business and governmental world, he will appear as a king, with all the authority, speech, etiquette, and order that is expected and accepted in those areas of life. To the spiritually inclined, he will function with the words, actions, and purpose expected in those circles. Nonetheless, the love, compassion, mercy, wisdom, discernment that are the very evidence of the King's Presence within are clearly present in the ambassador no matter where he is sent. Unlike the traditional roles of men, ambassadors of the King are always ambassadors; they are always representatives of the King, regardless of the setting they find themselves in.

This ambassador, then, has a dual role. He lives before God as a priest but before the world as a king. In his dual role as king and priest, he cannot fit into traditional religious molds. To do so is to miss the purpose and true function of these New Covenant offices. They belong neither in the religious system nor the secular government. They transcend both.

Because an ambassador of the Kingdom is trained by the King, he has spiritual attributes that are not usually found in earthly governance. For instance, an ambassador-king has the discernment to understand the spirit in a room and can also tell with whom the real power rests in that room. A king with this vision is always at least a few steps ahead of the crowd.

Jesus, the Enigma King/Priest

Jesus, our King, is a great example of this. More than just a few steps, He was light years ahead of the crowd! Consider how He demonstrated His Kingship in the highly politicized environment of Roman-occupied Judea. Remember, this occupation was an affront to almost every Jew and a daily reminder that they were far from God's intention for them. During the larger general era of Christ, the Jews generally divided into a handful of "camps" as they sought various ways to deal with the occupation. Yet Jesus did not fit neatly into any one of these camps. No wonder they did not know how to receive Him! He was an enigma to them.

Unlike the zealots or would-be messiahs, Jesus did not fight against the occupation by taking up arms and planning revolt. He didn't withdraw from society as the Essenes. He didn't compromise with the ruling system for his own profit as the Sadducees did. He didn't retreat into prideful religious legalism as the Pharisees did, looking down their noses at society. As a Master of Heaven's purpose, He sidestepped every single category! He could not be boxed in by any group. Scripture makes it evident that for some time, the Pharisees were trying to figure out if He was on their side. After all, He *was* closest to them doctrinally. Both the Pharisees and Jesus were concerned with the holiness of God being expressed through His people, and it was a central part of both of their teachings. But where Jesus differed from the Pharisees was that He elevated the love and forgiveness of God on equal standing with His holiness. This was more than the Pharisees could bear. Because He fit no easy categorization, eventually all these groups turned against Him and rejected Him.

Unlike our Lord, religion today is *far* too easily categorized into one or more of the same sort of groups. We are completely predictable in the eyes of the world once they figure out which "camp" we fall into. May God give us grace to go beyond the crowd and defy the easy categorizations of our day!

One knows he is successfully fulfilling his role as Ambassador of the King when he does not fit neatly into any of the existing boxes and belies the creation of a new box just for them. Although there is an acceptable box. That box is *Christ-yielded*.

Emerging Kings from the Secrecy of His Presence

As men and women become more aware of His Life within them, they are more acutely aware that man's ways are clearly not the ways of his Lord. His own ego becomes a glaring obstacle to the ways of his King who dwells within him. These emerging kings become appalled at the rise of their own fleshy retorts and humanistic gerrymandering for the expediency of a particular group. He is finding that he cannot stray from the heart of the King, for his heart has been renewed with the heart of the King. The demands of his selfish heart are now the enemy of his deepest desires. He will never execute a policy under the guise of spiritual correctness when it clearly does not resonate with the purposes of the King whom he claims to represent. These priests of His Presence are a new kind of ambassador, for they do not just represent the wishes of the King, they are kings to nations. As the writer of Hebrews explains, "And He is the radiance of His glory and the exact representation of His nature, and upholds all things by the word of His power" (Heb. 1:3). All things hold together by the words of the King, not by the words of him who would claim to act in His stead but does not live the authentic lifestyle of the King. Some seem to not get it. The King is not looking for folks to act like Him. He is in search of those who will die to their egotistical pride, selfish ambition, and personal kingdoms to be part of something much bigger than they that is eternal, peaceful, compassionate, and authentic to the deepest part of their hearts.

Jesus was not just referring to the poor when He said, "Truly I say to you, to the extent that you did it to one of these brothers of Mine, even the least of them, you did it to Me" (Matt. 25:40). We are able to excuse our actions when we interpret this passage to mean only the poor and disenfranchised. In reality, He was establishing the principle that Christ dwells within all men and women, and the extent that we submit to Him is the extent to which the world sees Him in action to the healing, the transformation of the world. In actuality, true citizens of His Kingdom are lamps through which the King shines. Yes, He has prepared a lamp for His anointed. That lamp is you and me.

The King's Wisdom

When you know your assignment, you know what you can do. We are not limited by how God has made us. We are limited by who we believe ourselves to be. Personally, I have come to discover that I can do all things through the King who strengthens me. Because the King lives within, I can do whatever needs to be done. Titles, positions, even education can limit us. But the King made us to be conduits of His Life. If the King can do it, I can do it, for the King lives and has precedence within my heart. When Henry Ford opened his first factory to make the Model T car, the press loved to goad him about his lack of education as he never finished high school. At a press conference, a reporter asked him, with an obvious sneer, what his degree was in. Ford replied that he had a degree in everything, for he simply hired in whatever expert he needed. He knew there was an answer at his fingertips for every challenge he faced. He was aware of his limitations but was not discouraged by them. He had sources for everything. So do we. Our lack of expertise, wisdom, even faith does not discourage as we have the King Who gives us of His everything as we are humble enough to ask Him.

The ambassador-king is discerning. His role is not religious in the marketplace, though he may have religious training. Truth is, it is not so much your education that qualifies someone for a position; it is the yieldedness to the King that opens doors for us the world over. The ambassador is a person who can be anything God needs him to be. For instance, in business he is there to make a profit, not to be a spiritual leader. Yet the principles of love, mercy, and righteousness are always at the forefront of his thinking. He therefore becomes a spiritual leader by his actions toward all men. The same can be said for those in government, the media, education, or whatever field one may be in. You will always win when you remember that you need the moment-by-moment wisdom of God to be successful, to win, to prosper in any field. For the wisdom of Solomon is not a product of years; it is a gift of God. It is actually harder to have godly wisdom as you get older as the tendency will be to draw on the wisdom of the past rather than the wisdom of God.

Authority Through Character

The authority of the King is true authority. Although our culture is one of appointed authority and assigned control over another, it is not a sure thing that those in authority have earned the respect they have over those they rule in one capacity or another. Those who have not earned respect by fair work practices, compassion, and encouragement ultimately exert authority with intimidation, fear, and uncertainty. Unearned authority is dangerous as it is unproductive. Ambassador kings/priests will thrive in even the most difficult environments as they allow the character of their King to shine through them. This, then, is what sets them apart. They understand that brute force, threats, and heavy-handed control does not work over the long term. Their goal is to earn the love and respect of those they serve.

Ambassadors Toward All

We are ambassadors of His Kingdom to all the peoples of the earth. When the nations look upon an ambassador, they should see the country that birthed them, raised them, and trained them. Everything about them should speak of the sending country. True Kingdom ambassadors have decreased that He might increase within them. The passion is to be a worthy representation of their King. To that end, they live sacrificial lives, not getting entangled in the affairs of the country to which they are sent. They are in a foreign country but they are not of that country. If an ambassador forgets that simple distinction, he has forfeited his position, influence, authority, and honor. He disgraces the home country and minimizes the global authority of his country.

The King decreed long before any of us were born that the individual carries a destiny, a purposeful contribution that is essential for the earth to prosper and flourish as the King intends. These ambassadors are singularly focused on that end and understand their mission to direct and in many cases redirect folks toward their contribution to the world.

It is clear that a brand-new generation of Kingdom ambassadors will need to emerge throughout the earth, raising the bar of personal responsibility and inner governance. Selfishness, evil speech, and war may gain attention, but they are short-lived indeed. Without moral integrity and genuine love for his fellow man, the ambassador of any nation loses the respect of those who count on him. Honor lost is difficult to regain. Nonetheless, there is a generation of King-sent ambassadors who renew the hope of the world in the power, possibilities, and prestige of the Mountain of His governance.

Influence

One can quickly tell those who influence others and those who do not. Those who influence others are not merely repeating the talking points of a particular group or movement. They speak as they themselves have researched, experienced, lived. These are the voices that change a culture. They are strong in their positions and can articulate their views with new insight, refreshing thought, and calm, peaceful assurance. Like Paul, these folks die daily; therefore, everything becomes new every moment.

Those who do not influence but are the victims of suppressive influence live in the shadows of yesterday, of religion, of tradition, of a politically correct mindset whose goal is to cement society in a way of thinking that can be controlled and manipulated.

And do not be conformed to this world, but be transformed by the renewing of your mind, so that you may prove what the will of God is, that which is good and acceptable and perfect (Romans 12:2).

*"Behold, the former things have come to pass, now I declare **new** things; before they spring forth I **proclaim** them to you." Sing to the Lord a **new song**, Sing His praise from the end of the earth!* (Isaiah 42:9-10)

Awareness of the King's Presence

As discussed earlier, the true priesthood of His Presence, the order of Melchizedek, lives in the Presence of God. They carry, as a normal experience of their faith, a lifestyle of conscious awareness of His compelling Presence. This is unique indeed. It is an incredible combination of brokenness and power, weakness and resolve, doubt and confidence, fear and assurance. His Presence reflects absolute dependence on Him and absolute certainty of His Life pulsing through the ambassadors' veins. It is exhilarating and frightful, natural and very much supernatural, manifesting through meekness but unlimited power. The awareness of His manifest power does not, as one would imagine, make one dominant, overwhelming, or arrogant. It does not being out our worst but gives us the possibility to bring out His best through us. His Presence is not a gift; it is the result of Divine desire and is the product of broken repentance. These folks understand that they have nothing to give if they do not give Him Who is within. They have discovered that reducing their faith to a mere philosophy reduces their Redeemer to the level of other social experiments and puts them on a level playing field with all others who vie for the attention of humanity. The difference between this priesthood and other methods is that they actually serve and dwell in the Presence of the Living God. This Living God also lives within them. This reality cannot be overstated and cannot be dismissed. He Himself is the Divine King Who is on a mission of His own. That mission is to bring the tranquil, compassionate, healing atmosphere of heaven into time and space.

At first observation, the introduction of yet another religious movement on the world scene would strike fear and even revulsion into the hearts of most men. I understand that. Many terrible things are done in the name of religion. It would seem that there is no apparent difference between the religious and the secular. There isn't. Both are equally unable to rule with the good of all men as the driving force of their governance. Even worse, secularists rule with open shamelessness in their repression of the people. Religion does the same thing only in the name of their god. History is filled with the good intentions of men of faith that have resulted in the most horrible of events. Every religion has had its awful stains throughout history. There is none free from guilt.

To be sure, any reference to these most regrettable times in history can be appreciated and the subsequent caution expected. But we must understand the stark difference between what man has done in the past and what God's purpose really is. Once His heart of love and compassion is seen and understood, anything contrary to Him is easily identified and rejected. Our King is not interested in the seats of secular government; He is passionate about the seat of man's heart. His plan is, as it has always been, to win the man. When the heart of man is won, everything around him changes. If someone is in government then the government changes. If the person is in business then the business changes; if in education, education changes; if entertainment, then entertainment changes and so on. When man fails to experience a heart change, laws are enacted to force people into an attitude of obedience. The law is indeed an inferior substitute to the inner governance of the King.

Many Christians attempt to legislate a change of action in lieu of a change of heart. They think that by placing godly men and women in office, they can achieve the governance that suits their moral and ethical compass. But the centuries have shown that this does not happen. A nation can be strong-armed into a certain behavior only to be released from it at the next election. It is a sad commentary on human nature, but it is one that is completely predictable. Human nature tends to revert to its base instinctive behavior and worse.

On the other hand, those who believe in the inherent good of humanity and ignore the foundational principles of the King are equally unable to bring about the utopian society they are so certain can happen. The point is simple—inner governance by the King is the antidote to the ills of society, any society.

The obsession of some religionists to focus so heavily on secular governments here and abroad is an aberrance to the authentic message of the King's heart. Those who center so strenuously on the rule of secular law have yet to understand the purpose of the King within them. At the end of the day, it is the individual He wants to woo and win for Himself. There is no separate nation, no culture, no community set apart for the man. The Kingdom He builds is within, and the connection of each of us is Spirit—a bond that, unfortunately, few comprehend. It is this spiritual bond that creates a force for good in the earth that restores the peace that the King is so committed to on the earth.

Yes, the King wants to woo, win, and transform the man into a priest so that, as a king, the man will transform the culture and then the nations. The transformation must begin in the heart, where hopes, dreams, and possibilities spring up. A man who is forgiven, a man who is loved is free to imagine, explore, invent. He is compelled by what he is experiencing in his own heart to love as he is loved; to forgive as he has been forgiven; to encourage, bless, and give even has he has experienced the same of the King who has done the same for him.

Make no mistake about the Life of which I am speaking. This thing cannot be faked. Words are not the indicator of what is happening within a person. Mere confession no longer is enough. Words, no matter how sweet, how perfect, will never convince our skeptical society. We have only ourselves to blame. History has proven words without constancy of action mean nothing. Actually, it may be argued that words alone would alert the discerning that something is off-kilter, for sure. Many have the right words but have not followed through what they have professed. It does not matter the eloquence of the words spoken, the number of Bible verses quoted, or the title one carries. There are none more incensed at the flagrant lack of integrity in every leadership level than those who have made the commitment and the sacrifice to be to this world what the King intends for them to be.

The work that the King is doing cannot be duplicated. It cannot be manufactured by human understanding. I will say it again. The absolute reality of His manifest Presence cannot be faked. The union of word and demonstration of His Life in the individual will change the world because it changes individuals. Those who are given to Him have no personal agenda, no political ideology, and no desire for personal fame. They are indwelled by Him, changed by Him, led by Him. They live in surrendered brokenness and their joy is to see Him exalted among humanity. While it is true we are all in process, we allow the Light of His Presence to show us the yet-hidden things that we abhor. The perfection of our actions, while not as within our grasp as we would hope, is exactly what keeps our hearts ablaze. Brokenness is a lifetime friend as we walk softly, circumspectly throughout life. Nonetheless, I have no other ending to this story; the King has promised a people who would be conformed to His Image and manifest His Life—the Sonship of God in this life. Those foolish enough to believe will undoubtedly get the closest to achieving it.

His mighty love arises within His people. He is sovereign. He is engaged. He is consuming. His Presence shuts the mouths of His detractors. This Kingdom and this King will not be marginalized either by political expediency or religious ecumenism. His Kingdom is established in the heart or it is not established at all. His reign is not from the top down. It is from the inside out. He wins the hearts of nations one heart at a time. He works through everyday folks who have committed to allow His simple reign within. In the "yes" of the King, they are true instruments of change, for their radical commitment to inner transformation reflects the Person of the King and His relentless love for this planet.

True Love

The language of this union, this priesthood is the language of true love—true, unconditional love. It is a love that gathers those so many others ignore, heals those who are the outcasts, and loves those who have never felt or experienced the reality of true love. True Divine love is evident to those who are governed by the King. In fact, the Light that shines so brilliantly from the His Mountain is Divine love. When ordinary people are submitted to the Divine brilliance of His love, they become extraordinary indeed. This love is anchored within; it affects all who come in contact with it. It attracts all who see it. True love heals and restores all who bask in its warmth. It can never be overstated—if the life of one who claims to be governed by the King does not reflect that inner governance, he is not being honest.

The nations do not want a religion or the language of religion. They have seen the reality of what man has labeled *religion* and promised in the name of religion. They have heard religion's promises and watched on in disappointment as it failed miserably in the demonstration of what they believed so intently, so completely. It is no wonder that the King has been rejected. He has been sorely misrepresented, misquoted, misinterpreted, and misused to justify the most horrific of actions.

But global government has not done better. Evil men, whether secular or religious, cannot govern righteously without the inner transformation of the King. The litany of their failures would take equally long to discuss as those on the religious side. All human governance fails as it tries to rule their own mountains by imposition of external rules and codes of conduct. Conduct cannot be righteous; actions will never be altered without a genuine change of heart.

The love that is born in the heart of the King, true love, will always give birth to righteous policy, holy commitment, and inner determination and desire to please the One who has done such a marvelous work within their own hearts.

I Surrender All

Surrender, then, is the basic true love-response to the King's work within. Surrender is the evidence that love actually exists between two people, between the King and man. It happens naturally in an environment of trust and mutual respect. "Mutual respect?" you ask. Yes, mutual respect. God respects how He made us. He respects our free will and refuses to tamper with it. He is confident that He can win the world with true love. The fact that this has not happened—after all the years, all the money, meetings, Bible studies, conferences, ministry schools, and sermons—is a glaring indictment of our inability to adequately demonstrate our love to a desperate world that is looking for true love. But whether human or Divine, love is the ultimate goal of all human experience. When surrender is practiced, love is nurtured. It grows. It is perfected. It is, in fact, the peace that passes all understanding.

Yet, many are taught to ignore this most precious response to the King. We expect Him to love us so much that He acquiesces to our vulnerabilities, our sin, and accepts us permanently exactly how we are, with no anticipation of change or realignment of loyalties, actions, or desires. Yet we expect Him to be the One who meets our needs, to bless us regardless of how we live. Saint Paul had quite the revelation when he wrote that God blessed the children of ancient Israel because they were His children, in spite of their rebellion and resistance to His plan for them. God cared for them but was not pleased with them. They had sentenced themselves to endless wanderings in the wildernesses of uncertainty, fear, confusion, aimlessness, and poverty. Yes, they never went hungry, but neither did they prosper. They were in His heart but out of His will, far from their destiny and far from the love relationship the King so desired to have with them. The Promised Land was reserved for those who would, after all, trust Him enough to lay aside their fears, their vulnerabilities, their doubts, and respond to the command to possess the Land of Promise.

Religions teach to fast, claim, decree, rebuke, resist, and meditate. We are told how to dress, how often to go to religious activities, and how much to give. We are told how to believe, how to pray, and how to live a holy life.

Governments tell us what we need, where we should live, and how we should eat. They demand far more than the religious tithe but give far less. They talk with holy indignation and then do in secret what we are condemned for even thinking. They choose our words, our schools, and try to tell us when life begins and when it ends. They have exalted themselves, just has the religious oligarchs have done, as those who know better than the rest of us. Yet failure, famine, war, and every form of evil flourishes. We need the King.

The Elephant in the Room

The missing ingredient is the elephant in the room that seems to be blatantly ignored. They are missing Him. Whether secular or religious, they are missing the key to the fulfilling Life most of us actually crave. Few understand that He is waiting for man to lay down himself that he may take up Christ, the King, His Kingdom that is the Mountain of the House of the Lord. Few are ever encouraged to surrender, to repent, to lay down their own will in order to take up His Life. I know it is not politically correct to believe someone has to change their behavior. It is even becoming less religiously correct to teach true heartfelt, life-changing repentance. With the current wave of political/religious correctness, humanity will continue to go down the path of self-destruction, obliviously ignoring the reality of their grievous philosophies.

Ignoring the very essence of union with the King will only prolong the pain. In fact, we really need to stop turning our faces from the reality that is happening all around. Man must simply surrender. Yes, the surrender is to Him. He is not surrendering to us. We are to become like Him. He came to earth so that we might be redeemed from ourselves to the radiant Life of Divine love that is intended to saturate us body, soul, and spirit and then affect all those around us. We become windows to the Divine, dying to the fleshy ways of our carnal nature to be clothed with Him—wrapped, as it were, in His glorious light. We, therefore, become like Him Who is pure, spiritual, overflowing with love, compassion, and peace.

The King changes our minds, our actions, everything that is not in harmony with His Life flowing from us. It is little wonder that we are admonished, "We are destroying speculations and every lofty thing raised up against the knowledge of God, and we are taking every thought captive to the obedience of Christ" (2 Cor. 10:5). The only way to be a Divine window to the world is to change. The only way to change is to repent, surrender, die to our human way of thinking, acting, judging.

> *For the love of Christ controls us, having concluded this, that one died for all, therefore all died; and He died for all, so that they who live might no longer live for themselves, but for Him who died and rose on their behalf* (2 Corinthians 5:14-15).

> *If anyone is in Christ, he is a new creature; the old things passed away; behold, new things have come. Now all these things are from God, who reconciled us to Himself through Christ* (2 Corinthians 5:17-18).

Each individual must take the time to know Him. Otherwise we become more religious, more dependent on men than before. One cannot be told what to surrender to and what to resist. There will always be those who are happy to tell you what to do, how live, where to go, what to fear, and who to love. But the teacher is the King who dwells within. He is the One who etches His laws on the heart. He teaches, guides, and empowers. A person's softness of heart as well his willingness to be redirected and rediscovered are keys. When we do not allow our ego to resist new thoughts, we are on the road to finding the discernment of Spirit that truly leads to true love.

> *A new commandment I give to you, that you love one another, even as I have loved you, that you also love one another. By this all men will know that you are My disciples, if you have love for one another* (John 13:34-35).

Here is the point. A true discerning heart will not be easily convinced by the words of others, no matter how eloquently spoken he might be. Position, popularity, or the success of a man will never replace the discerning heart as the ultimate arbitrator. True ambassadors of the King must have the discernment of the King. They are not adolescents; they know what they know by their attention to the One teaching them. Of course, teachers will always be teachers. But in the end, it is the individual who must have the wisdom and discernment to either accept the words of another or not. The responsibility is theirs, and the authentic citizen of His Kingdom is happy to carry that responsibility upon themselves.

This is a prayer that I often find myself praying: "Dear Jesus, give us a heart of true spiritual discernment so we might cooperate and not resist Your mighty plan. My dearest Lord Jesus, teach me *surrender*."

CHAPTER SEVEN

Priests of the Mountain

Priests Toward God, Ambassadors Toward Man

The paradox of "priesthood" adds to its mystery, its allure, its role in the Kingdom that begins within. This priesthood, descended from Melchizedek, has not merely existed throughout the millennia, it has lived in victory throughout the millennia. It is the reference point for all that the King conquered when He gave Himself for the redemption, the restoration of mankind. The Mountain of the House of the Lord is the heart of this priesthood already living in the victory He secured. Hence, that priesthood is the resurrected Man within, yearning to give expression of His Life to every person.

Appearing quite mysteriously to Abraham, Melchizedek was recognized as Priest of the Most High God. His priesthood could not be changed, was not affected by death, was eternal in nature. It is a priesthood in Spirit and in flesh. Abraham immediately and without question tithed to him, recognizing his position as both natural and eternal. Eternal in the sense that man could not overcome or defeat it and natural in that this priestly Life is to be expressed through all those who would surrender themselves to Him in loving devotion, singularly worshiping Him and offering themselves to Him without resistance or argument. The great and victorious, loving and powerful, gathering and compassionate Priesthood would be a portal, as it were, through which the world would see, understand, and experience the wonders of the King Himself.

From the beginning until the end, the purpose of God for man was singular. He wants a priesthood through whom He can love the world as only He can in kindness, mercy, peace, and wholeness. It is not in the nature of man to put others first, to seek the good of all in spite of the obstacles, to be the servant, the giver. Maybe that is why our King saw fit to rule through the likes of difficult and resistive folks like me. We must voluntarily, consciously, and decisively reject our self-centered, self-preserving nature to allow the King to do what no man can in himself. We have the possibility at our disposal to be the priests of Melchizedek, the throne of the King, the Lamp of the Anointed, the city on a hill, the Voice of the Beloved, the portal through whom the world may gaze on the wondrous King. He is calling mere mortal man to be transformed into the image and very likeness of the King, who *is* the Mountain of the House of the Lord.

And you shall be to Me a kingdom of priests and a holy nation. These are the words that you shall speak to the sons of Israel (Exodus 19:6).

And they sang a new song saying: "You are worthy to take the scroll, and to open its seals; for You were slain, and have redeemed us to God by Your blood out of every tribe and tongue and people and nation, and have made us kings and priests to our God; and we shall reign on the earth" (Revelation 5:9-10 NKJV).

Transcending Man and Spirit

Therefore if anyone is in Christ, he is a new creature; the old things passed away; behold, new things have come (2 Corinthians 5:17).

The Lord says to my Lord: "Sit at My right hand until I make Your enemies a footstool for Your feet." The Lord will stretch forth Your strong scepter from Zion, saying, "Rule in the midst of Your enemies." Your people will volunteer freely in the day of Your power; in holy array, from the womb of the dawn, Your youth are to You as the dew. The Lord has sworn and will not change His mind, "You are a priest forever according to the order of Melchizedek" (Psalm 110:1–4).

This priesthood transcends religious and governmental boundaries. Melchizedek stands before God as a priest, transformed, instructed, directed, and possessed by Him. The priests of this order live in the Presence of God in loving worship and sacrifice, knowing that the work of God within them has been the result of their decision to present themselves to the King daily for their role as ambassadors before men. This inner governance is the essence of His Kingdom, for through them Christ the King lives His own eternal Life. They have made covenant with the King of the Mountain of the House of the Lord. They surrender self-control to King-control. From the deepest part of their heart, they are committed to the inner governance of the King.

> *For this Melchizedek, **king** of Salem, **priest** of the Most High God, who met Abraham as he was returning from the slaughter of the kings and blessed him, to whom also Abraham apportioned a tenth part of all the spoils, was first of all, by the translation of his name, **king** of righteousness, and then also **king** of Salem, which is **king** of peace. Without father, without mother, without genealogy, having neither beginning of days nor end of life, but made like the Son of God, he remains a priest perpetually* (Hebrews 7:1–3).

The dual role of Melchizedek is distinctive in two ways. He is a priest before God. He gives himself to God moment by moment for transformation, instruction, wholeness, strength, peace, courage. He is a priest before God that he might be prepared to be a king before man. So both traditional definitions of the roles of king and priest require redefinition, fresh understanding. We cannot fulfill what we do not understand. We cannot understand what we cannot allow ourselves to reexamine.

The approach of this priesthood to God is one of humble repentance, openness, holy reverence, and sacred worship. That is, we stand before Him abandoned, silent, ready to be renewed in every way as we yield our argumentative, prideful, and self-seeking opinions. In this priesthood, there is only Him. There is no compromise, no rebuttal. His priests made ambassador-kings are expressing the King's love with all His holy, wholesome, and encouraging attributes. They are compelled with the desire to see all men made whole, fulfilled, and of absolute necessity making their contribution to the world as the King has always intended. These folks are made before God but they serve among man.

The reality and function of the Melchizedek priesthood is more different than any other priesthood or governance created by man. This priesthood is ordained by God Himself, for Himself, and is the last of the three priesthoods established by God in ancient Israel. The first two were temporary and were intended to fulfill a role until the eternal priesthood of Melchizedek made its entrance into time and space by the King. His role was to be the One who faced death on behalf of all mankind, thus making the way of kingship for all men.

The Calling of the Kingdom's Priesthood

All who have called upon the Lord have the possibility, even the right, to participate in this priesthood. Of course, actually fulfilling that role depends upon dedication to the King and the willingness to live in broken repentance. But this destiny is written in humanity's spiritual DNA. The capacity for such devotion as a Melchizedek priest is within all, and such ability is ready at the surrender of the man.

Melchizedek allows God to be Himself through him in order to reach mankind. This representation of the King places a profound responsibility on the earthly priest to relinquish control of his will and his own ways so that God, in turn, can express Himself to humanity through men and women, mere humans transformed by the work of the King Himself. This eternal Kingly expression is to reveal the very nature of the King to a dimensionally imprisoned race of beings who have forgotten their origin and have either abandoned their place as kings and priests of God or they have sold themselves out for a more self-serving lifestyle. These people fall drastically short of why they were called, redeemed, and given breath.

It follows, naturally, that if God so purposes a complete expression of Who He is to this planet, He would redeem for Himself a people through whom He might fully express the power and vastness of His love. True priests of the Presence, what the Bible calls the "priesthood of the believers," always have His interests at heart. They always love first, forgive first, are the first to gather, the first to recognize their own lack, and the first to point the way to the King so that the world sees the truest expression of God's unfailing and eternal love.

The Priest of the Mountain of the House of the Lord

The role of a priest of the Lord's Mountain is much different from the traditional role of a priest, minister, or pastor. Traditionally, these folks were the intermediaries between man and God and then told them what He expected of them. The folks were always an arm's length from their God, as in the Old Covenant mere mortals could not come before God. This understanding comes from the ancient Hebrew laws contained in Judaism. Under this religion, ordinary man could not approach God and live. God was holy, pure, could be angered, and was quick to repay lawbreakers. This was the avenue to show humanity what life would be like without the redemptive work of the King who took His Father's anger and our sin upon Himself to bring the two together in a harmonious union of mutual love and respect. God respects our will; we respect His Lordship.

Most religions and denominations still maintain that the priest is the intermediary, the one who cushions the blow from God for man. They teach that their role is to be the padding, the protection, the discerner of truth for the people. But when Jesus died on the Cross, the curtain of the Most Holy Place, the area of the ancient temple in Jerusalem where the Presence actually dwelled, was torn "from top to bottom." Jesus completed that work long ago; now there only remains the fellowship of man and King in an inseparable union of Life and vision. The only intermediary needed now is the Christ of God, the King of the Mountain of the Lord, Jesus. This is essential when we understand that the King did not come to start a religion; He came to establish a Kingdom within the hearts of all who make room for Him, allowing His governance to overtake them.

When God sent the King to the earth, He sent the King to redeem mankind so the law would be fulfilled. In short, He gave all men the possibility to be priests to God. He forgave their sin, cleansed them from their penchant toward sin, filled them with the Presence of the King for the purpose of changing the heart of man so that they would, by nature, surrender themselves to God. Because of what the King accomplished on the earth, all men could now not only approach God but have fellowship with Him. Not because man was perfect but because he was redeemed from the consequences of the law. Now man could approach God with confidence knowing that the blood of the King covered man's imperfection until the power and love of the King was able to change him. By presenting themselves to the King for inner transformation and governance, man would be empowered and changed by the very Presence of the King within.

The King's priests are of another priesthood. They stand before God to offer themselves as agents of change by changing themselves first into citizens of the Mountain of God. By becoming sacrifices to the King, they are able to accurately allow God to live His Life through them. But the end goal is not to create a priesthood class for the people to interact with. The end goal is for each individual to come before the King and offer himself as the Order of Melchizedek did for thousands of years.

This priesthood lives in the Presence of the King. It is there that the priest is taught, surrenders his weaknesses, discovers his strengths, and walks in his destiny. He gladly admits his shortcomings and relinquishes them to the King. The last thing these priests want is for their weaknesses in this life that are contrary to the ways of the King to stain the reputation and purposes of the King. In short, they do business with God so God can do His work through them on this planet. The priest then proves the reality of the King's work on the earth by living the life that demonstrates the inner transformational power and governance of the King. The attesting lifestyle, when it is authentic, naturally becomes the salt that makes others thirsty for that same relationship with the King.

If the Life of Jesus is studied from this perspective, it becomes easy to see how Jesus walked the earth as a King before man and always a priest before God. Jesus had the authority to forgive the sins committed against the Father of the Kingdom. He had authority over the wind and waves. Demons had to obey Him. He could walk on water, walk through walls, and raise the dead. The authority of the King is evident in everything He did whilst on earth. At the end of His earthly mission, He passed His authority on to those who would follow Him. Those who would be ambassadors of this Kingdom would carry the same authority as does the King, for the King indwells the priest. In the same way, the attributes of the King, what many call the fruit of the Spirit, are the oil, as it were, that makes the will and authority of the King flow so freely through them.

Lifelong Transformation, Lifelong Fulfillment

Although brokenness is the key to an authentic life, most see it as a real negative. But brokenness should not discourage us. It should not make us sad or destroy us. As a priest of God, brokenness is essential. Brokenness makes us pliable, teachable, humble, useful. Brokenness is empowering. Brokenness is not crushing. It makes us priestly conduits of His Life, love, and compassion. Every true priest of God is touched by the weakness of others. Brokenness helps him to carry these ones in intercession rather than judgment.

He can have compassion on those who are ignorant and going astray,
since he himself is also subject to weakness (Hebrews 5:2 NKJV).

For we do not have a High Priest who cannot sympathize with our weaknesses (Hebrews 4:15 NKJV).

To be sure, the process is lifelong but the rewards are in the present as our broken repentance cause us to be a continuous flow of His *everything* to the earth through the likes of average folks like you and me. To live is Christ, to die is gain—not just gaining the reward of heaven but fulfilling your destiny in this life. The King's determined desire is for us to live in *now*, experiencing the vastness of the possibilities He has prepared for us. Tomorrow belongs to Him.

We should never fear Brokenness, for she comes with the will of God gently (if we can accept gently, otherwise she comes as a battle axe) showing us the error of our way and lighting the path for our journey. The limp of Jacob was not a weak, embarrassing, or humiliating visual. It was a constant reminder to him as well as a constant reminder to those who saw him that encountering God is a life-altering event that should be desired every day. When Brokenness is planted in our hearts, destiny cannot help but grow, the King cannot help but be seen, and His Kingdom cannot help but be established within.

This is where the will of God is founded, explored, displayed, and fulfilled. The heart of man is the key to everything. You would do well to give Him all of it.

Godly Brokenness

Jacob wrestled with God. Although the Scriptures say that he prevailed, he lived the rest of his life with a limp. The result of his wrestling match with the angel left him broken. It was the kind of Brokenness that reminded him who was in charge but still gave him the power, the resolve, and the wisdom to do the right thing. Some folks are broken in spirit, having been through circumstances that they should have never had to face. This brokenness leaves a person in deep emotional pain and is not at all what God has intended for us. The King's love does not permit emotional abuse. Spiritual, emotional, or governmental abuse cannot happen through those who claim that the King's governance dwells within them. Remember, if the fruit of the King is not clearly evident in a person's life, then the Life of the King is not the controlling power within.

The breaking of the King in our lives yields love, life, and glorious fulfillment. But the destructive ways of man will destroy a person forever. Do not confuse the two. The abuse of man is not the breaking of God. One should know which he should resist and which one he should embrace. In either case, when you turn to God as your refuge, the evil actions of man can be turned into something that God can use for your benefit. The more we dwell on the destructive actions of others, the more we are crushed instead of broken. Some live in the attitude that everything we don't like, don't believe, is not convenient, or disrupts our comfort zone cannot possibly be God. But we do not know Him as we should if that is our belief. God is after our maturity, our surrender. He will do what He needs to bring that to pass. Those who do not see this will spend their lives resisting the very purposes of God for their lives. The priests of the King are acutely focused on the Life of the King within and are keenly aware of their shortcomings. Therefore, they are not so quick to rebuke, pray against, resist, or blame others for what is happening to them. They look deeper, get quiet. They want to gauge their reactions, understand their responses so that they can see if there are ways within them that still need to be given over to the King. Their goal is to see every circumstance as redemptive, every trial as a positive transformational opportunity, every roadblock as their King intervening for a particular reason. These priests of His presence know how intimately involved He is in their lives and they are committed to cooperate with Him, regardless of the trial. They have grown past the fleshy argument of who is right and who is wrong. Their more fundamental question is, "What should I learn from this?"

It is amazing what is really under our personal control. Truly, life and death are in the power of our decisions. We are more than we have been told we are. We are more than we have believed our-selves to be. The power of the King within will withstand all the torments of man. More importantly, the power of the King's inner governance will bring us to a place of fulfillment and destiny that we have never dreamed.

> *Grain for bread is crushed, indeed, he does not continue to thresh it forever. Because the wheel of his cart and his horses eventually damage it, he does not thresh it longer* (Isaiah 28:28).

The Mountain of True Love

The King's priests are grown on the Mountain of the Lord. The priesthood is not established by majority vote, military conquest, or international negotiation. Remember, mountains in Scripture simply represent places of authority. When Micah says "the mountain of the house of the Lord will be established as the chief of the moun-tains" (Mic. 4:1) the prophet is seeing that the authority of God will become the chief place of authority and it will be so influential that the nations will stream to it. But is Divine authority the expression of Divine love? What does God do apart from love? He does nothing. His authority is directed by His love so that all that is seen from the Mountain of God is the expression and fulfilling mandate of Who He is—Love. In the same way, the focus of these Christ-yielded priests is not primarily the response of the people to whom they are sent but the motivation of the King within. They are not interested in trying to find the religious thing to do; they merely want the Christ of God to actually live His lovely, supernatural life through them. They have died to themselves. Their lives are hidden in the King, who is hidden in God. Their personal preferences are immaterial. They are dying to them. They desperately want only one thing. They want the King to live, love, gather, heal, restore through them with no thought for personal glory or political advantage. Godward, they are personal friends with Him. Toward the nations, they are King-servants so they can serve His mighty Presence to the nations.

When the Presence of God is flowing through those who call themselves ambassadors, the Divine Nature is evident to all. Paul lists the fruit, the evidence of the Spirit.

> *But the fruit of the Spirit is love, joy, peace, patience, kindness, goodness, faithfulness, gentleness, self-control; against such things there is no law. Now those who belong to Christ Jesus have crucified the flesh with its passions and desires. If we live by the Spirit, let us also walk by the Spirit. Let us not become boastful, challenging one another, envying one another* (Galatians 5:22–26).

Here then is the banner of those who have truly made a covenant with Him by sacrifice; not that there is any other way to make a covenant with God, but there are many who will alter the terms for their own advantage.

Where Do They Come From?

Although university, Bible school, and other such institutions can prepare the mind, only God can transform the heart. For it is not *what* you know that will make you a functioning priest of His Presence; it is not even *who* you know. The question is more simple than most we have ever asked. Who am I yielded to in loving trust and Divine union? A casual acquaintance with God or an intellectual or religious assent to His existence is far from adequate. The mind cannot wrap itself around the magnitude of the King.

That is fine. The intellect was never intended to be able to comprehend His love, His compassion, His single-minded focus upon such a fallen and depraved race as ours. And yet we are to love Him with all of our heart, mind, and strength. Thus yielding ourselves to be renewed in our understanding so that we have the mind of Christ. God knew that the salvation of humanity was not in its ability to solve world-ending problems. Humanity's salvation would be, in its desperation, to call upon the One Who holds in His heart everything needed to gather humanity together into spiritual and natural union. The priests of Melchizedek have discovered that the hope of the world is in the mind of the King. That means His plan, His wisdom is the very solution we seek. Our ultimate surrender gives room for His ultimate wisdom to rule through those who will allow Him access to their hearts.

The effect of this union with the King would most naturally flow into time and space bringing peace to this troubled planet. Surely, the King's first earthly visit magnified the need for His Kingly rule in the planet. Little did many understand that that Kingly rule would be by Christ the King through those who have learned to live in broken repentance before the King and before man. But this Brokenness should not be misunderstood. For meekness is not weakness, and the lifestyle of Brokenness and love should not be confused with the very real need for personal accountability and responsibility. The very nature of love requires a demonstration of all love's expressions, all her desires, and all her fulfillment. Love does not exist in a vacuum, nor can it be reduced to a cheap thrill or simply a meaningless ecumenical term intended to appease the aggressor and comfort the victim but producing no lasting transformation.

Wholeness Brings Restoration

Wholeness brings restoration, and restoration inevitably brings change. This is the hope that world craves. It is a hope that this God, Whom we say is so powerful, will not leave the world in its broken state. True hope has little desire and even less time for a grace that tries to make one content in his condition. The world wants the grace carried by the priests of His Presence. They want the grace that will forgive, heal, restore, and gather to newness of Life. They are tormented by inner pain and want deliverance from it, no matter what it might take or might mean. I know this from personal experience.

As a devout Catholic, I (Dr. Don) went to confession again and again, desperately wanting to be forgiven for the destructive lifestyle I knew I was living in. No matter how the priest would tell me the things I did were not sin, I knew better. I knew for I felt the pain of separation from God and there were no words that would comfort me. There was no precept of the church that would give me rest from my torment. Then I did the unthinkable. I approached God for myself, on my own, naked and ashamed, with the burdens of the world and torment of sin hanging from me. I cried out to God with the desperation of a condemned man, for I was. It was there, on that fateful night over forty-five years ago, that I was forgiven. I had experienced the Scripture, "For all have sinned and fall short of the glory of God" (Rom. 3:23). But that day, I also experienced the Scripture, "If we confess our sins, He is faithful and righteous to forgive us our sins and to cleanse us from all unrighteousness" (1 John 1:9). This is not a poke at Roman Catholics; I happened to get a priest with a humanistic view of right and wrong. The point is that a person knows when he is not right with God, and no amount of political correctness or redefining Bible principles will change the inner torment of separation with God. Only the individual knows whether he or she has been forgiven and is right with God.

There is only one priesthood that connects the individual with the King because the King Himself is the first Priest of Melchizedek. That priesthood exists in the Presence of the King and has prepared a place in His Presence for each one of us. No other priestly activity results in union, peace, hope, and destiny. Other priests prepare the man for the part of their inward journey. Melchizedek is the fulfillment of the journey and the eternal ministry of the King in the earth.

I am describing the emerging Melchizedek priesthood and it is unlike any other. It does not have the convenience of personal opinion, does not have the luxury of personal prejudice or historical bias. For this priesthood, the only passion is loving as He loves. That means there is nothing that can trump the Life of the King as He shines through them.

It then becomes easier to see how this priesthood does not simply proclaim Life. They are not even exclusively intercessors. They are doers, listeners, responders to the Voice of God alone as they hear His Voice within and are submissive to His will. They have learned the discernment to separate their humanistic tendencies from the will of God. They recognize human emotion and Godly zeal. They can separate the pressures of men from the leading of the King. They know His voice in the flurry of voices that shout their opinions, their prejudices, and their prideful self-serving solutions.

Their lifestyle shows that there is a force at work within them that the world cannot reconcile, explain away, or even deny. These priests, male and female, demonstrate, prove the Life within by their actions and attitudes, desires and passions, motivations and words. No wonder Micah cried out concerning the emerging Light of the King in these last days:

> *And it will come about in the last days that the mountain of the house of the Lord will be established as the chief of the mountains. It will be raised above the hills, and the peoples will stream to it. Many nations will come and say, "Come and let us go up to the mountain of the Lord and to the house of the God of Jacob, that He may teach us about His ways and that we may walk in His paths." For from Zion will go forth the law, even the word of the Lord from Jerusalem* (Micah 4:1-2).

Once again, it is the King's attributes that prove the activity of the King, nothing else.

Thus, the emergence of this priesthood will be and is a result of desperately hungry folks laying down their own limited intellect to embrace the mind of the King in Whom are hidden all the treasures of wisdom and knowledge. It is difficult for most to accept, but it is nonetheless true. If man was capable in himself, surely he would have, by now, figured out how to live in harmony with one another and gather everyone into community that loves, nurtures, and encourages folks into their full potential. History proves that man cannot do it, no matter how he tries. Pointing the finger at one group or another only magnifies the lack of human ability to secure lasting, positive change in an individual, let alone a culture.

Union with God

Union is a word that is central to authentic Kingdom citizenship. Nonetheless, it is strategically ignored by the religious as well as secularists, probably because genuine *union* with the Divine is the end of tyrannical secular and religious governance and intimidation. As we discussed before, genuine inner governance changes a person from within. The rule of the King looks nothing like the inconsistency of kingless governance. The rule of the King is the end of religious and secular control with their false moral premise of human invincibility. *Union* with God is the end of religious, Pentecostal parlor tricks and legalistic, religious hyperbole that impresses few and leaves most convinced that the King and His Kingdom cannot possibly be the answer. The world is desperately looking for a valid expression of the faith proclaimed by someone, anyone who says that they have the solution to the debilitating issues for which humanity appears to have no answers. If the world is to stream to the Light that shines atop the mountain of the Lord, it will be because some have adequately demonstrated that their King has the answers that truly forgive, gather, heal, and transform. This answer cannot be presented as a list of principles or even a program that is adequately funded and administered. It must be presented as the only way it can ever be believed, accepted internationally. It must be lived. It must be seen as working in the crucible of everyday life, whether one is a suburbanite in the U.S., an urbanite in London, or a struggling villager in the Sudan or Chile. The nations stream to the light that works, that offers solutions, that demonstrates wholeness to all in pain, sickness, and sorrow. If that light fails, so does its influence. There is no other way.

These priests of the King do not just live in the cloud of His Presence. This priesthood is the source from which the cloud of His glory flows. Their moment-by-moment submission to the will of God, their second-by-second response to the subtle nudging of the King is union that causes the fire of His Life to glow so brightly. That union consumes all that resists His mighty plan within their hearts. The conflicting forces of the inner man will war until we give over our will to His will, our desires to His desires, submitting our plans to His destiny. Union is truly the fire of consistent, predictable Life. Our dying fleshy resistance to Him is the fuel that burns and creates the Light the world runs to. That unquenchable fire releases the glory of the King, the cloud of His Presence that carries the essence of His mercy, the reality of His grace that gathers, heals, transforms, and plants hope where there was no hope. Union with the King is not the goal of life; it is the tool, the preparation, the beginning of the restoration of His love, the healing of humanity's pain, and the visible display of eternal love on planet earth. The fruit of our inner life is the constant plumb line—our guide, as it were, to be sure our decisions, our words, are those that build, heal, gather, bring peace, and ooze with the love of the King. To be sure, our lives are often the antithesis of what we are committed to living. Therefore, a reflective life attitude of broken repentance will keep us in touch with our emotions, our desires, and our motives. A lifestyle of dependence on the King will consistently point us to Him. Any thought, attitude, or doctrine that does not reflect His attributes, His personality should be seen as a place for repentance, surrender, and ultimately change. The simple rule of thumb? Love rules, compassion drives, mercy gathers, and hope does not disappoint.

Union is not initiated outside the man, but its effects burst forth from within those who are living in broken repentance. The outward glitz and glitter of man-made fanfare is not so necessary when the fullness of His Life-experience pulsates in the depths of one's heart. Union is the ultimate assurance, the end of the argument, the convincing experience that His love is eternal, His mercy is abundant, and His compassion never fails.

Union with the King declares by living example, "I and the Father are One." It is the visible, not verbal proof that the answer to the depraved human condition lives within those who will give themselves to Him in humble and broken repentance.

This, then, is the gathering of the people, the healing King, the loving King, the only King. This, then, is the end of human struggle and failure, sorrow, and pain. It is the beginning of trusting Him Who lives from within, originating from a dimension that few have seen, fewer have experienced, and even fewer believe exists. This is where the Mountain of the Lord's House is fulfilled. Its spiritual GPS coordinates mark the heart of man as its location. The Light of man's Brokenness flowing from its peak proves its holy governance is truly working.

CHAPTER EIGHT

The Challenge of Outer Governance

Outer governance is the rule imposed by one man onto another. It is the premeditated, forced control of actions, attitudes, activities, and beliefs by a person, religion, or government without a corresponding, voluntary, inner change on the part of those being ruled. I know of no governing body—religious, business, national, or local government, cultural, or societal group—who does not rule in this fashion. It is the accepted method of controlling the people. It is so ingrained in us that most will balk at this statement.

It is not that outer governance may not be necessary; it is that without an inward commitment to the rule of another, an inward change of heart, outer governance is doomed to eventually fail. Its hollow proclamations and promises, patterns and purposes are spoken by untransformed hearts to be adhered to by untransformed hearts. How can it possibly succeed?

Simba was a little cub when he discovered his destiny. He would someday be the king of the jungle! All the land he could see would one day be his kingdom. He was destined to be the boss, the chief, the head honcho, the CEO, the president, the top cat. He was so excited and so proud. He was eager for everyone to know, and so he was quick to strut about his newly discovered destiny.

What Simba did not understand was that governance on any level—whether it be a prime minister, a president, a company CEO, a dad, or king of the jungle—was going to take a change so deep within that would change his actions without forever. Simba had the revelation of his future but had no clue what it would take to get him there. He was just too young to understand that leaders are not born, they are made in the crucible of daily struggle where men change in a way that makes them a great leader. The alternative is to resist the process and go down in history as just another wannabe in a long line of those who thought they could rule with their own wisdom, lead in their own strength, and build under their own power. Yes, Simba was about to find out what it would take to be a mighty king, and he was about to discover if he had the courage to make the toughest decisions in his life.

Well, Simba is a character in a Disney cartoon, but the lessons are as real as it gets. There are countless "Simbas" in the world, and all want to be king without the process that will make them great leaders. The roads these folks take will determine just what kind of leaders they will become. Yes, their decisions will determine their contribution to the world or their drain on the strength and vitality of those who are in their care.

> *And he said to them, "The kings of the Gentiles exercise lordship over them, and those who exercise authority over them are called 'benefactors.' But not so among you; on the contrary, he who is greatest among you, let him be as the younger, and he who governs as he who serves"* (Luke 22:25-26 NKJV).

Outward Governance

Men love to rule others. It gives us such a sense of superiority. Every time a person exercises control over another, he feels empowered, godlike, even invincible. But this sort of feeling is an indicator of an inability to be a leader. Yes, outward governance is a mirror of what goes on within. The genuine, the soft-hearted, the broken hate its every appearance. They are quick to surrender that bit of arrogance to the King so that He may rule. For outward governance is what this is all about. When one is given the opportunity to rule—whether it be in his family, a business, a religious organization, or a nation—the truth of who that person really is becomes evident. His outward governance shows the world who is ruling his heart. It is to this issue that the King has given His Life. The question that determines the peace of the people is simple: "Who rules the heart?"

Men make decisions, either consciously or unconsciously, according to their deepest held beliefs, their most powerful traditions, their most hidden passions, desires, and fears. In short, man rules others the way he rules himself. He reacts to circumstances that are firstly self-preserving and secondly self-serving. The breakdown of all national and international woes is summed up with these observations. Men rule others to their own advantage. It is a fact of life but also a fact of our humanity.

Any sober-minded individual will have to admit that after all we have discovered in science, all we have invented, the technological advances we have made, the intellectual sophistication we have achieved, all the books we have written, and all the laws the world has passed, humanity is still spiraling downward in a chaotic malaise for which nothing we have done has worked. True to human nature, we have blamed everyone whose philosophy, religion, or form of government differs most from our own. We have convincingly accused, chastised, rebuked and condemned, not realizing that all of us are spiraling down together. It takes a very honest and courageous person to turn the accusatory finger away from others and center it on the one most responsible for the state we are in. Yes, it takes a very brave person indeed to be willing to look within himself. Once we dare venture a peek, we see the forces of self, hate, prejudice, and fear that drive most of our decisions and form our way of living and governance. Like Walt Kelly said when he famously paraphrased a wartime dispatch in 1813, "We have met the enemy, and he is us." It will require humility, for few there are indeed who are willing to truly see themselves and their weakness apart from their King.

By now, I am sure you can understand why governing anything or anyone is so difficult. Even with the best intentions, most will fail given enough time. The passions of the heart cannot be controlled forever. Man does not have the strength to overcome his very human, very earthy instincts that have ruled and condemned us since that fateful day when the first apple was plucked from the tree in our first act of Divine disobedience. That act did not release something new within us; it revealed the very nature of humanity that was never intended to rule himself or anyone else for that matter. Man was created for union with the King through Whom humanity would rise above himself and his penchant for steering everything toward his own benefit. That original design has not changed, no matter what the current trends promote.

Dr. Don's Experience with Outer Governance

As a publisher, I started out with very specific standards and work ethics. I created rules of operation to protect the vision of the company as well as the people who worked for me. I was committed to personal and business integrity in all my operations. Nonetheless, I was amazed at the many temptations to do things that would be an advantage to the company but not so good for others. I remember time and time again sitting alone in my office when something crossed my desk that would be financially successful even though it was morally wrong. I was alone. No one would see me or even know about the unscrupulous means with which I could make more money. In normal human thinking, it would be called a "win, win." I would get what I wanted (win number one) and no one would ever know what I did to secure the contract (win number two). In reality, however, before God it was a "lose, lose." I would have violated my business ethics in my own eyes and in the eyes of God (loss number one) and I would have cost someone else the contract that was rightfully theirs (loss number two).

When such an opportunity would arise, I admit that the temptation was there. Sometimes it was strong. I would feel myself being worn down by these temptations as well as the needs of the company. I nearly convinced myself that a bit of deviance was acceptable as long the company benefited. It was, after all, a ministry. It would help secure the future of the company as well as secure the economic welfare of many people. When bills piled up, it seemed that the opportunities to stray from my commitments relentlessly challenged me. I was wearing down. There was no doubt about it.

Then came the day a man approached me hoping to buy into the business. He had prayed. He had fasted. He had thought through things very carefully. He was certain he was making the right decision. Although his offer was not a lot of money, it initially seemed as though it could be a good move. I approached my prayer closet forgetting—more accurately, ignoring—what God had spoken to us when Cathy and I started the company. I conveniently forgot that God was "looking for a prophet to publish the prophets," that the call was specifically on my life and the lives of our sons. I seemed to ignore the fact that God has placed a mantle of trustworthiness and confidence on us that drew many authors to us.

So when I went to prayer, expecting a long time of waiting and listening, I was shocked to get my answer before I got my first prayer completely prayed. There would be no waiting, no more praying, no discussion. His answer made that quite clear without ever expounding. God simply spoke to me, "The anointing is not for sale." Okay, then. Wow. I was embarrassed at my apparent greediness and hunger for expansion and greater visibility. I was angry at myself that I had allowed myself to ignore all that God had instructed me. I was ashamed that I had so devalued my calling that I was willing to sell it. I had to repent. In that awful yet wonderful time of turning my heart back to God's heart for me, I realized that at that point of repentance, I had died to the hope of building a huge company. From that time onward, I focused on the Presence, the authors, and the books even more intently than before. He had called me to this. He would provide or I would go out of business. I marketed, advertised, and sold books with only one goal in mind. I would publish the prophets with all the strength and wisdom that God had given me. I would do right by the authors, respecting them and respecting the message God had entrusted to them. I would not entertain building a personal empire or establishing a name for myself. Although I had published a few books of my own at that time, I refused to promote them in the fear that I might exalt my own work over another person more worthy than I. Only after I handed the company over to my sons did they begin to market my books vigorously.

Why Does Failure Come?

I knew that I was being watched by Someone far bigger than me and far more capable of resisting or exposing any devious plan I might try to create. But there was something else at work within me far more important than that. I *wanted* to please Him! I wanted to make Him proud. I wanted to be all He wanted me to be. But the fleshy desires of mortal man are no contest to the powers that are at work in the earth that would woo, lie, and do anything to sidetrack me from my deepest desire.

Then I realized something I had never considered. I fail because I want to succeed in my own strength. I work to do what I think is right, the way I want to do it and when I want to do it. I am trying to do the work of the King in my own strength. Christ within me is my hope. I cannot do it alone. I cannot live it alone. I cannot fight the temptations alone. I cannot make the right decisions. I cannot do any of it alone, but He can. He will. He wants to! What a relief when I first came to that stunning realization. It was at that point that I met Brokenness and began the journey to the inner governance of the King.

The only way to keep myself from evil was to die. Yes, I would have to die! Not physically, of course, although some are martyred for their faith every day. I speak of the death to self-will, that pride-powered ego within that needs to rule, control, command, and win at any cost. It is that part of us that will resist surrender, resist the opinions or instruction of others. It must maintain dominance even in the face of obvious failure. Often, the more we resist, the more obviously we are exposed as inadequate.

At some point, we must recognize that the more we resist, the more apparent our weakness is to others, if not to ourselves. The soul of the man must, if there is to be authentic growth, begin to reflect, in his life, the condition of the spiritual man—dead yet alive, fallen yet raised again. That death is as real as physical death. However, it is usually incremental. But it is, nonetheless, dying to the things that want to draw me away from my beloved King. He reigns where I give Him opportunity. He rules where I die. He takes over as King where I surrender.

The apostle Paul was so adamant about staying right before God that he told the world that he died daily. He was not ashamed to admit it. He lived in an attitude of broken repentance. The "broken" part gave him the courage and humility to daily confess his weakness. The "repentance" part was the determination to turn from it, to die to its influence over him.

This lifestyle keeps the Life of the King vibrant within. It keeps me from needing to make excuses for my failures and frees me from the guilty accusations of the enemy of my soul. This is the heart that can hear the Voice of the Lord. When the heart is quiet and free, He can be seen and heard much more readily. God does not play games with us. He is not trying to make life difficult. I make life difficult when I refuse to surrender to the King and resist the death to elementary things of this world that are bent on distraction, derailment, and destruction.

Brokenness does not make us sad; it makes us pliable. Brokenness is empowering. Brokenness is not crushing. It makes us teachable for the rest of our lives. To live is Christ, to die is gain.

When the righteous rule, the people rejoice (see Prov. 29:2).

The Key to Sustained Success

When you accept, when you understand the goal of the King within you, the days become joyful, refreshing, fulfilling. You become the effective, natural leader He made you to be. It is forever true—outward governance, either of ourselves or of another person, will ultimately fail.

When Peter denied the King at His most difficult hour, he was sure he had forever lost his place with the King. He ran, much like we do when guilt and self-condemnation overcome us. Even though Peter had walked with the King for three years, he still did not grasp His love and could not see a future for himself in the service of the King. The King knew what Peter did not understand. Nonetheless, he was about to get a glimpse of the depth, the commitment, the determination, and the destiny that the King carried in His heart for mere mortal man.

"Feed My sheep," the King said to His friend when He saw him at the seaside. Peter would have none of it. He knew he had failed. Peter condemned himself, judged himself not ready to serve. Peter had seen himself. His words were arrogant and his actions were predictable to everyone except Peter. He knew he had let down the One he so desperately loved and wanted to please. He would never fail Him again. Surely he had disqualified himself.

"Feed my lambs," Jesus persisted. Yes, He was in Peter's face. But Peter needed to see Jesus's love for him. Peter was drowning in his own regret, however, and he hated himself for it. I doubt Peter felt he would ever be ready to walk alongside Jesus ever again. I am sure Peter was disgusted at his own inability to make the most difficult choices. No, Peter knew he had no strength to back up his mighty claims. He knew he was finished.

One more time Jesus spoke directly to Peter. "Do you love Me?" Peter's eyes must have caught the gaze of His Lord. The thought of Jesus still wanting him, still trusting him, still believing in him was more than he could endure. When Peter's eyes met his Lord's, I am certain that the love of Jesus flowed as freely as a waterfall into his heart. That love broke through. It changed Peter's mind, changed his focus, and forever cemented his resolve to surrender his will to the purposes of the King. The King's expression said a million things to Peter. I can almost hear the Voice of his Lord loving, assuring, gathering Peter back where he belonged, back where destiny would prepare him for a future he would have never predicted.

I am certain Peter wept as he heard the heart of his King toward him. "Peter, Peter!" I can image His words. "You have failed because you have mistaken your work! You thought your work was to change yourself. But, My dear friend and brother, that is My work within your heart. Your work is to change the world whilst I change you. Peter! You stick to your calling and keep your heart open as I do My work within you. Ha! We will work together. Now, get back into town and do the will of your King!"

The Heart Does Not Change by Itself

True ambassador-king outer governance has costs. For most, at least for now, the price is far too high to pay. This is largely due to us knowing the price we pay by maintaining control of ourselves and all we touch. But as more people take that initial step of surrender to the King, more will see the overwhelming proof that permanent change is possible, even inevitable for those who die to themselves, their egos, their politics, their religion, and even their ethnicity. The rise of the King from within the heart will display a new way of living. It is what the ancient prophets called the "new song." It changes everything from our speech to our actions and attitudes. This is where outer governance truly begins. It begins within the human heart.

This so simple and obvious, it is a wonder that more have not spoken of it as the necessity that it really is. Personal destiny cannot be tapped, individual contributions to the world are not seen, tolerance is never replaced with love until the King truly is given the freedom to rule the human heart.

Yet we continue to institute programs that do not touch the heart. We pour money into a problem instead of love into the heart. A nation is not empowered by money. A cursory glance at the U.S., Great Britain, and many other rich countries belies the notion that money, human intellect, or science alone are the answers. The heart is ignited by purpose, not programs. Potential is released by genuine encouragement. Love is the force and passion that ushers in personal destiny and accomplishment that benefits the world community.

It is way too easy to speak without imparting Life. It is too easy to strut about with authority and great oratory skills. For sure, these can stir the emotions and engage the passions of the listeners. But when daily or weekly talks are needed to continue to stir a person to commitment and submission, then the heart is not being challenged to true inner submission and change. Long-term outer governance is achieved as men and women discover the Life within and begin speaking, not in their own wisdom, not their own agenda, but the wisdom and will of the King. The masses will follow a genuine heart, a compassionate heart, one who puts the well-being of the people before his own. This kind of person can be trusted. This kind of person can be believed.

Every individual is valuable. Everyone is a gift to this planet. It is the role of outward governance to secure equal opportunity, thus assuring that everyone has the possibility to add their value to society. It means everyone must discover his gift, his reason for being here. But it is the responsibility of the one to whom outward governance is entrusted to secure that opportunity to develop their potential for the good of society. To do this effectively, the heart of the leader must be free from all forms of prejudice. There is no place for political, religious, ethnic, national, economic, tribal, or arbitrary class discrimination. The heart of the truly inner-governed leader loves with the love of the King, who sees all equally and offers all the opportunity to succeed. The duty of government is be sure the opportunity is available to all who strive to better themselves and those around them. Authentic outer governance is the result of authentic governance by the King, and He offers Himself to everyone.

Can you imagine a world where everyone is seen as having a significant contribution to the earth; where everyone's contribution is encouraged, recognized, and celebrated? No one would be marginalized, ignored, or left behind. No one would be seen as insignificant. This is truly how that world is visibly transformed for the better with each passing generation.

The good news? This is the will of the King for this planet, for you.

No longer do I call you servants, for a servant does not know what his master is doing, but I have called you friends, for all things that I heard from My Father I have made known to you. You did not choose Me, but I chose you and appointed you that you should go and bear fruit, and that your fruit should remain, that whatever you ask the Father in My name He may give you (John 15:15-16 NKJV).

All authority has been given to Me in heaven and on earth. Go therefore and make disciples of all the nations, baptizing them in the name of the Father and the Son and the Holy Spirit, teaching them to observe all that I have commanded you; and lo, I am with you always, even to the end of the age (Matthew 28:18–20).

As the Father has sent me, I also send you (John 20:21).

Remember Who You Are!

Most don't believe they make much of a contribution to their family, not to mention the world. Most live in doubt, denial, or self-destruction. But that is not who you are, it is not how you were made, and it is not the will of the King within. There is no doubt that you are more, much more than you have become. The words of the King must find their root deep in your heart and soul. Yielding to the will of the King becomes easier, even exciting and compelling when we understand His destiny for us as an individual.

Outer governance will be surrendered to inner peace as you allow yourself to be convinced of the King's far-reaching plan for your life. When outer governance is replaced by the inner rule of the King, everything and everyone around you is changed. In this way, the world around you begins to change, beginning with you.

CHAPTER NINE

Changing the Conversation

Keep thy heart with all diligence; for out of it are the issues of life. —Proverbs 4:23 KJV

The good man out of the good treasure of his heart brings forth what is good; and the evil man out of the evil treasure brings forth what is evil; for his mouth speaks from that which fills his heart. —Luke 6:45

God spoke clearly to Ambassador Rivers early in his position as ambassador, "Every government on earth is represented except Mine." Of course, most would say a statement like that is quite ridiculous. But when you understand that the Kingdom of God was never intended to be a religion, it is not so ridiculous or radical. The Forgotten Mountain, the Kingdom of God, was always intended to be the rule and reign of King Jesus in the hearts of all men on the earth. Yet that thought is an anathema to most. Unthinkable in light of the Bible being recognized as a religious document and all its adherents members of a religion. But that was never the intention of God when He sent His Son to establish His Kingdom among men. According to those who now dominate the conversation, hasn't history proven the inability of this King to speak effectively among men? Haven't the followers of this King themselves disqualified the Bible as anything truly supernaturally loving and compassionate? It is difficult to argue to these points on an earthly plane. But this King is not on an earthly plane, nor are His ambassadors responsive to the controls of this natural realm.

If the King and His Kingdom are to be seen and understood as the formidable power for good that they truly are, then His citizens must arise as a truly righteous expression of the Kingdom. Who would want to be part of a movement that stubbornly holds to policy that is not expressed in personal, governmental, or business lifestyle? The King and His Kingdom are marginalized at best—outright forbidden in the marketplace of ideas at worst. The fault of this must fall squarely on those who claim His inner governance but live like those who do not know Him. Only the truest expression of His Kingdom through His own citizens will change the conversation.

The greatest *coup d'état* in history remains to this day. The world disqualified this Kingdom based on the apparent failure of its followers to show convincing proof that this inner governance is both authentic and beneficial. The actions of those who have claimed to be representatives of the King have made the acceptance of this governance nearly impossible. Predictably, the community of nations is convinced that they do not need God. Most refuse to admit the obvious. The further He is marginalized, the further we fall as a race. Man is a remarkable creature. He is both creative and destructive. He has abilities far beyond his understanding, yet he is unwilling to yield to the One who put the creativity within man and has the desire to release it. Man is strong but stubborn. He is certain he has the answers but is too stubborn to admit when he has reached the limits of his own understanding. He is both forgiving and ruthless. He forgives himself but won't give an inch to others who make similar mistakes.

This duality within is a struggle that man is doomed with unless and until he is willing to yield to the greater governance within—that is, Kingdom governance, the rule and reign of the King in the human heart. Many have tried to rule as the King but without the inner governance of the King. They have tried to respond with love of the

King but without the Divine love of the King that flows effortlessly, consistently, and predictably from the heart. The result has been a catastrophic failure to accurately represent the King as He truly is rather than as man assumes He is. The King is not like man; otherwise, it would not be necessary to surrender our heart to inner governance. His work within our hearts changes our minds, our outlook, our treatment of our fellow human beings as we begin to see as He sees, love as He loves, forgive as He forgives, and transform as only He can transform. There is only one voice that will restore the nations of the world to the glory that the King originally intended it to have. That one voice is the voice of the King. The authentic certainty of the King's rule within is the change of our view of everything toward the heart of the King. Man cannot imitate it. It cannot be substituted with a similar voice, for His voice carries the determined, compassionate, and restorative love of the Divine Himself.

Wrong Voices, Wrong Conversations

The wrong voices have had the attention for too long. Whether those voices be political, religious, or cultural, they have steered the conversation in directions that have led us all down a path from which many agree it will be difficult to recover. Nonetheless, as long as these voices are allowed to dominate the conversation without being challenged, they will rule the heart of the world, taking it to its own selfish and man-exalted ends. The trend of this unchecked self-centered view will only be changed when average folks like you and me determine to allow the King to speak the words of Life. For the most part, folks do not think for themselves; they do not take the time or the energy to search out, on their own, who they will be or what they will believe. Most are happy to be told who they are and what course their lives should take. It is no wonder that those who direct the conversation are so certain of their positions. With only one point of view, the nations will take only the direction they have determined is best—for them.

In education we are told that the smartest and brightest are the ones who get the highest grades. In many cases, though, these are the ones who follow the rules and are willing to eat whatever they are fed. Are they really the smartest, or are they the best at memorization and conformity?

If our intellectualism is so evolved upward, why is the world spiraling downward? History shows that those who have changed the world do not always fit the molds we are told to fit. Some of our greatest scientists, inventors, mathematicians, and business leaders never finished their education. Some were thrown out of the most prestigious universities and some even rode the "short bus" to school. Education rarely promotes self-expression, personal creativity, critical problem solving, and spiritual development. We have become experts at producing mindless drones whilst touting their accomplishments, as though conformity to standardized testing and modeling is the true accomplishment.

Religion feeds us the proper ways to believe, pray, and live. Yet folks continue to leave organized religion in unprecedented numbers around the world. Systems fail and no one seems to notice. Maybe no one cares. Maybe, just maybe, it is exactly what they want. When someone rocks the boat—whether that boat be governmental, societal, or religious—the entrenched powers are shaken. Some topple. All resist.

Controlling the conversation, feeding the people a steady diet of what is so convincingly presented as truth, keeps the people in line. Most are unaware that their mental diets can be as destructive as their physical diets. As long as the people cannot discern among the mountains of information they are served, they will always be manipulated.

Death and life are in the power of the tongue, and those who love it will eat its fruit (Proverbs 18:21).

Blind Obedience

When I was eight years old, my twin brother, Ron, and I found a bird nest that had fallen from a tree in a thunderstorm. Three chicks, not more than a few hours old, were lying in the grass. Ron and I quickly gathered them into the nest and brought them into the house. They looked so hungry! I touched one of them and the little guy opened his mouth! He was too young to open his eyes, but he knew he was hungry. Foraging through the refrigerator, we found the perfect food for them—last night's meatloaf! It was meat, had some veggies in it, and could be easily crumbled into tiny pieces. By now, all three chicks had their mouths open, although their eyes were still closed. We happily dropped bits of Mom's cold meatloaf down the throats of the chicks. But before we were able to return them to the tree, they had all died. We were heartbroken! "Mom! Your meatloaf killed our baby birds!" We cried as we ran through the house looking for the evil person who made such poisonous food. Of course, Mom was not amused, nor was she sympathetic. We had learned a hard lesson that day, but I didn't realize how important it was until many years later.

Most people are like those chicks. They go through their lives with their mouths open and their eyes closed. They will take anything that someone is willing to drop into their gut. Most will not know what they have eaten until it kills them, steals their peace, or destroys their future.

It is time to change the conversation. It is time for folks like you and me to talk about the things that preserve destiny, release potential, and encourage creativity no matter the cost to our selfishly personal needs. The world awaits this kind of liberty, this kind of freedom. The conversation needs to be changed to the issues of accomplishment, personal pride, and fulfillment.

Ambassador Rivers recently spoke at an anti-bullying rally where he did not take the now-traditional and predictable drone of the anti-bullying movement.

Instead, he talked of potential, destiny, their inner treasures. The place was silent as he talked about purpose, hope, and rising above the distractions that make one need to bully. He was the only speaker to get a spontaneous, rousing standing ovation from a thousand students. He changed the conversation. He offered avenues of thought that were new, exciting, empowering; that helped those students see the treasures within them, within their grasp. The world does not know what it is waiting for, but it is clear the world is waiting for someone to change the conversation.

Dr. Don was asked to speak at a youth conference on the dangers of sin. He spent thirty minutes talking about vision, calling, about the dream God had dreamed for them. He told them that they were destined to succeed, to win. God had created them for His purposes on this planet. When the talk was over, he was swamped by those who wanted to talk more, shake his hand, and ask him for prayer. The audience was thrilled, but it was not the conversation the leaders, in their minds, were expecting. He had changed the conversation from a list of hell-threatening "do nots" to a spirit-releasing presentation of what is within their grasp if they simply say "yes" to Jesus.

It is time to change the conversation.

Dr. Don's wife, Cathy, was assisting at a huge prayer rally on the Capitol lawn in Washington, DC. She was not there to do anything more than just help the scheduled speakers and organizers on the platform. The speakers each had thirty minutes to pray their burden from the King. Most spent twenty minutes promoting their personal ministries, then concluded with a few minutes of prayer for their work and then the nation. The attendees were only marginally involved as the day went on. Then, quite without notice, one of the organizers asked Cathy to go to the platform and take a thirty-minute spot as one of the speakers did not show up. Cathy would have had much to say. She was CEO and founder of Rachel's House, our local crisis pregnancy center. Cathy and Dr. Don together had founded Destiny Image Publishers and were developing a television program for teens. Yes, there was a lot she could have talked about.

But when she got to the podium, she lifted her hands heavenward and the glory of God flooded her. The people responded with a shout of worship and the familiar groan of intercessory prayer rose quite spontaneously. In what seemed like only a minute, she felt a tap on her shoulder that her time was up. She changed the conversation. Mountains were moved. Hearts were revived. God expressed Himself through a willing vessel. She could no longer walk among the people as she had been doing all day. She had changed the conversation, and now everyone wanted her to pray for them, counsel them, and give them a hug. She had briefly become a celebrity by what she did. Although Cathy had not intended to speak that day, she was accustomed to listening, waiting for her Lord. She simply yielded her heart to will of the King within. He changed the conversation.

What Needs to Be Said

It is no secret. Words are powerful. Thought is formed by our words. Attitudes are imbedded in our minds by ideas expressed by words. Conversations steer nations. In a moment, the world is changed. Concepts are challenged. Sacred beliefs are discarded. Individual words are redefined. Suddenly, the world is different—most often, different toward a governance of permissiveness and lawlessness among individuals on one hand, yet producing a tighter grip on the control of the population in general on the other hand. As long as there is no true King-led pushback, the spiral downward will continue, and those leading the efforts will be emboldened to continue on their systematic anti-Christ path.

Those with true Kingdom inner governance cannot be so easily dissuaded. The laws of the King are written on their hearts. Their minds are set. They represent not themselves but the One who has sent them to be ambassadors. Their words, their attitudes, indeed, their actions reflect the King and the truth of His Kingdom. Their speech is far from the daily rhetoric of those who are the self-appointed mind benders on behalf of society.

Enter the Ambassador-King

There is gold and a multitude of rubies, but the lips of knowledge are a precious jewel (Proverbs 20:15 NKJV).

Ambassador-kings speak from the heart of the King. They speak of hope and wholeness. They proclaim the Golden Rule and a way of living that allows all to fulfill their God-given destinies using their God-given talents to the good of all men. Their words truly gather. They are inclusive in the most traditional sense of the word. They do not teach a secular tolerance, but they are committed to Divine love. They understand the connection of all men as those created by a single God for a singular purpose. That is to see the earth and all her inhabitants living in a harmony that cannot be legislated from without but embraced in the heart. The policy of their King trumps their personal politics, usurps the authority of destructive practices, and sets the determined on the path of their own inner governance in the Kingdom of God.

Ambassadors of the King grow in courage and are resolute in their accountability to a power higher than that of mere mortal man. Because they are dying to their own ways, the words they use are not their own; rather, they speak the words of the King Himself. They are careful not to project their personal opinions; they see through His eyes and are baptized in His love, embrace His love toward all His creation, whether that creation be black or white, Muslim, Hindu, or Christian, Jew or atheist. His love transcends the finite powers of man and has as His ultimate intention the gathering of all men to Himself. His passionate love is single-minded, acutely focused on bringing all men to the reign of the King within, thus bringing true and tangible peace the earth in the daily experience of wonder and peace of His Kingdom.

Policy

It is clear that the one who influences the conversation will influence policy. He who influences policy steers the nations toward true global peace. This is seen in each individual who is not only recognized as having a contribution to the planet but is educated, encouraged, and otherwise empowered to fully make their contribution to the common good of all mankind. When the citizens of the Kingdom speak the words of the Kingdom with wisdom, love, and discernment, the conversation changes to the words of the Kingdom and true peace can begin to be seen in the earth. There is no doubt that the vast majority of folks are looking for a change in conversation, a change that will restore hope, opportunity, and destiny to them individually and nationally. In short, policy needs to change. But the conversation that changes policy cannot be full of religious platitudes or exegetical concepts that are not understood by the average person. Conversations that become national or international movements cannot exclude a person based on ideology, religion, politics, ethnicity, or any other discriminatory position. The key to lasting change, tangible hope, and permanent peace is getting humanity to the place where the King Himself can be the primary influencer of inner transformation and governance. As in any true diplomatic endeavor, face-to-face encounters always produce the best results. Ambassador-kings have impeccable trust in their King and His ability to bring wholeness to anyone who will meet Him. They understand that the King can do for others what He has done for them, to them, and in them.

Injecting personal opinions and working private agendas are not on the hearts of these emissaries from the King. Fleshy, human interference will only delay the mission of the King. The key to successful, outward governance is successful inner governance of the King.

Patterns of Conversation

The pattern of the conversation that engages the population must come from the King Himself. When the King walked the earth,

His words were religion-free. He spoke with definitive clarity as He moved among the people He came to liberate. The average folks spoke of the wonder of His words. His words were as compelling as His Presence and the miracles performed among them. Consider how the people spoke of Him:

Never has a man spoken the way this man speaks (John 7:46).

The crowds were amazed at His teaching; for He was teaching them as one having authority (Matthew 7:28-29).

Lord, to whom shall we go? You have words of eternal life (John 6:68).

Some of the people therefore, when they heard these words, were saying, "This certainly is the Prophet." Others were saying, "This is the Christ" (John 7:40-41).

Did not our heart burn within us, while he talked with us by the way, and while he opened to us the scriptures? (Luke 24:32 KJV)

The miracles got the attention of the people, but it was His words that captured their hearts and finally got Him crucified. Yet the pattern of speech was a pattern of love, compassion, mercy. His passion was authentic and His warnings were delivered with the expectation of repentance and change. He spoke with wisdom, discernment, and confidence. He was meek but not weak. He was determined but not ruthless, encouraging but not compromising. His words were liberating but never condescending. He resisted the proud and spoke out against the corruption of the faith as well as the hypocrisy of the religious. He loved those who hated Him, washed the feet of one who would betray Him, forgave those who nailed Him to a cross. He was the first God-Man, and He did not speak what He did not hear His Father speaking. Therefore, His words were precisely the ones that would save the sinner, heal the sick, gather the outcast, bring hope to the downtrodden, destiny to the hopeless, and peace to the world. Our words should do no less.

The words of the King will always change the conversation. They create a public discourse among those who seek a better, a higher way of living. But they must be spoken fearlessly and with the love of the King clearly evidenced. The selflessness of Jesus's words made Him safe to be around. The genuineness of His heart made Him trustworthy. The confidence with which He spoke gave the people hope. His only agenda was the one He carried from His Father. It is no wonder Jesus was able to change the conversation among a people so desperate for change. They knew that Jesus had their best interests at heart. He spoke words that gave Life to the soul.

His words carried no personal attacks. His talks did not condemn, separate, or accuse. In His love, He spoke of a Kingdom and its people. He spoke of how they lived, loved, and gathered. His words spoke of life, hope, and inner transformation. The listeners would either allow their hearts to be engaged by His words or resist His words so that personal change would not be necessary. But however His words were taken, they changed the conversation to a higher place of wisdom, hope, and possibility. No wonder He was loved by the common people but hated by those of the entrenched authority.

Misguided Guides

A national discourse is prompted by the media, who do it for profit. Special interest groups will steer the conversation to their very narrow soapbox. But the ambassador-king will speak words that take root in the heart. Their words plant possibilities and release the masses to once again pursue the destiny that the King planted within them. The words of Jesus reflect the patterns of conversation that can— that must—dominate the nations as the fate of billions of people is debated. It is the mission of the King's ambassadors to be certain that, whilst so many critical issues are discussed on an international platform, the words of the King provide the vibrant alternative to the downward spiral of our planet in spite of all the human solutions that are offered.

Religion parrots preach the sanitized version of the national discourse to preserve their own base of power and to maintain their profit. Their guiding words are a tragic misrepresentation of the King when folks who are the purported voices of the King merely echo the current trends of the secularist power bases. The only alternative to the dominating voices of humanistic reeducation is the voice of the King. He is not an echo. He does not wait to determine the popular trend. His goal is not harmony at any price, for He knows that there will never be such harmony without the determined change to the inner governance of the King. If authentic Kingdom citizens do not rise up with the attributes and words of the King of the forgotten Mountain, our civilization is doomed to repeat the failures of the past. Democracy is not the answer in itself. Science is not the answer in itself. Technology does not change the heart. Money does not bring inner transformation. The world waits for the conversation to change—your conversation.

Whoever influences the conversation has sway over the people. The King is actively looking for ambassadors who will begin to take the lead in the conversation for the benefit of all humanity as Dr. King did so many years ago.

Dr. Martin Luther King, Jr. changed the conversation as an ambassador-king. He did not come at a time of a critical change in the history of a nation; his conversation made it a critical time in our history by changing the conversation. Everyone says "gradual change," but he responded that more than 200 years was unacceptable and an excuse to keep things as they were. Sometimes change must be abrupt. Sometimes one must speak what few want to hear. Sometimes things never change because a situation will not be engaged. Sometimes someone must have uncommon courage, uncommon conviction to begin a conversation that no one wants to start. Only when a situation is engaged with compelling dialog can there even begin to be change.

Dr. King once said, "I often feel like saying, when I hear the statement, 'People aren't ready,' that it's like telling a person who is trying to swim, 'Don't jump in that water until you learn how to swim.' When actually you will never learn how to swim until you get in the water."

We have ignored the conversation of those who have been marginalized. So we lost the opportunity to engage in the conversation that restores everything beginning with the soul of man and ending with the soul of a nation. Our biggest failure is believing that those we discount are discounted by others, therefore we ignore them and what they say. Those who speak will dominate the conversation, lead the conversation, and therefore shape the thinking of the masses.

When you begin to change the conversation, be prepared for the onslaught of your detractors. Understand that if your detractors are focused on you or your point, you are successfully beginning to change the conversation and eventually the course of cultural and societal thought. This certainly is what true leaders do. You will not find authentic world changers saying what everyone wants to hear. They will say what needs to be said, void of the echoes of religion, politics, and selfish ambition. Yes, these folks stand out like a sore thumb to those locked in a controlled politic, either religious or secular, but their words are like music to the ears of those crying for love, freedom, hope, and true peace.

A man's words certainly define him. They express his thought, his passion, his desires, and his goals. Listen carefully to what is truly being said. More importantly, choose your own words carefully and be sure you are ready to engage those who resist you. Words spoken by the King are words that are irrefutable. At the end of the day, the only way to silence Him, the only way to rebut His wisdom was to hang Him from a tree. Thus, the power of His words among men become evident. Who is willing to be His mouthpiece in the gentleness of His love, the compassion of His desire, the evidence of His mercy?

It is the Spirit who gives life; the flesh profits nothing. The words I speak to you are spirit, and they are life (John 6:63 NKJV).

A Contemporary Manifesto?

A manifesto is a simple, public declaration of intention that is proclaimed by a political party, government, or an emerging group of influencers onto the public platform. By its very nature, the word *manifesto* implies a radical shift of ideas from the status quo. It implies a major upheaval of what has been accepted practice in society. A manifesto implies a head-on collision with the apparent foundations of the sacred pillars of governance and faith, the rules of engagement for war and peace, the understanding of global stability and human rights.

Manifestos often emerge at times of extreme political crises, rampant moral decline, or the unchecked collapse of human rights. When one or more of these conditions is allowed to continue by the powers that be, it is often the righteous who will rise up with determination and resolve to make right the wrong that is ignored, explained away, or—an even more sinister tactic—accepted as right when it is destroying the very foundations of life. A manifesto says to the world, "We have had enough, we have seen enough, we have waited, and we have given ample time to respond to the destructive forces of our world."

To be sure, it is not the writer but the reader who ultimately determines if the declaration can be truly deemed a manifesto. A simple rewording of a contrived outrage or the warmed-over solutions that have never really worked to stir neither the heart nor the imagination. A true manifesto ignites a spark within to either be a part of the solution or to resist it. Either way, the spark of true change will have been ignited and change will be truly in the air. Vocabularies are rewritten, motives are redefined, passions are adjusted, and purpose is put into motion. For once the fires of change are truly set ablaze, there is no stopping the march toward the kind of reformation that heals the nations, gives hope to the destitute, and sets men on a course of true restoration of body, soul, and spirit.

A manifesto is not just a declaration of what is wrong; it is a declaration what can be, what should be, what will be again. It is full of hope. It arises as the very conscience of a generation. It may offer solutions that have never been offered on the platform of public discourse, or it may be a call to return to the heart of what had been glory that once made the people hope, dream, create, invent, love, discover. For when the foundations are secure, the people are free to become all their DNA, both natural and spiritual, has intended them to be. The declaration of a cultural conscience brings exhilarating possibilities to all people, great and small, and makes everyone's destiny attainable, their futures bright, their lives fulfilled, happy, peaceful.

But the solutions brought forth will surely require radical change, personal responsibility, and genuine commitment to the common good of all men, not just the ones who fit my definition of "acceptable." Manifestos shout from the housetops that there is truly hope, that we are not doomed to failure, judgment, and destruction. Men and women with true inner governance and resolve will rise to the challenge and risk all they have accumulated, all they are in order to be that company of people who can, without question, usher in a time of genuine wholeness and peace to a tired, struggling planet that has no solutions, no direction, no future. These simple, genuine folks, with fire in their bones and love in their hearts, carry the torch of hope, the strength of possibilities, and the assurance that good, as embodied in a Man, is the change that redeems a planet.

Now if you are still reading this, there is a good possibility that you are at least curious as to what this is all about. It may also be that you are frustrated over what you were so sure was going to work but, sadly, has not. You may have heard the claims of many, took the steps they required, but found that they all lead to the same dead end you had always experienced. There is nothing more depressing than launching on a path of so-called "proven success" only to eventually discover that hyperbole does not bring hope or healing. Promises made are far from promises experienced. You have discovered that hope deferred truly makes the heart sick—sick and tired of trying the next big thing.

But now, it is not up to another. The hope of tomorrow is not in someone else's ideas. In the past, you had gladly taken the responsibility for your own actions, your own decisions to follow the plans of those who were certain they knew better than you, but alas, they did not. The Mountain of the House of the Lord, the King's Mountain, stands tall and formidable, mighty and authoritative, certain and undaunted. This Mountain is the permanent Home of the King of Glory. It is the storehouse of love, compassion, and mercy. It the place where hope is born, wisdom lives, and power flows freely. It is the Mountain of the House of the Lord and it is within you. You no longer have to wait for marching orders from someone who is supposed to know better. He Who indwells you knows better and has chosen to live within your heart. He knows better and is talking directly to you. The King is wrestling control of His people back from the hands of those who had usurped the King's authority in lives of those He has personally redeemed.

Your King is waiting patiently for humanity, for you, to quiet down, to silence the noise of mere mortals, to remove the distractions as well as the trappings of unproven processes. He is waiting for you. His heart is bursting with the very solutions you have prayed for but expected another to deliver to you. But I get ahead of myself. In the pages that follow are words you may have never read, concepts you may have never considered, a functional inner governance you may have never imagined was actually possible. It is no longer just possible; it is absolutely critical to the global recovery of wholeness, peace, and the prosperity of the whole man, to all men, for all men.

The rule of the King from His throne of authority, your heart, is about to burst onto the scene with all that He is, all He has dreamed for humanity, all the determination of One who gave His life for the likes of you and me. He is coming with Divine love, compassion, and mercy. Yes, He is coming. The King is appearing on this planet— through you.

If you are brave, I challenge you to turn the page on your life. I don't quite understand the following sentence. If you are frustrated with what has been, turn the page on your goals, on what you live for. If you want the King to be the master of your fate and captain of your future, move forward with this determination in your heart: "It is no longer I who live, but Christ lives in me, through me. The Life I live from now on is the sacrificial life of surrender to Him who rules from the forgotten Mountain, the Mountain of the House of the Lord within me."

Classic Wisdom on the Kingdom
by Myles Munroe

Heaven and Earth: A Clash of Cultures

Not long after national elections in the Bahamas, someone asked me in an airport, "What do you think about your new government?"

I replied, "I only have one government."

It doesn't matter who occupies the prime minister's chair or the Speaker of Parliament's chair or the governor's mansion; it doesn't matter who sits on the throne and is called king or queen. There is only one government, and it belongs to Him whose throne will never be moved or toppled—Almighty God, the King of kings and Lord of lords. His rule in Heaven is eternal, without beginning or end. But He also created the Earth and established His Kingdom there as well.

The Bible says, *"For the foundations of the **earth** are the Lord's; upon them he has set the **world**"* (1 Sam. 2:8 NIV). The words *earth* and *world* often are used interchangeably, but here they refer to two different things. *Earth* refers to the place, the physical planet on which we reside, while *world* refers to order or governing affairs. God created the physical Earth and then set on it the "world" of His government and divine order. *Earth*, then, has to do with location, while *world* deals with who is running things.

God rules directly in Heaven, but His plan for the Earth was to rule it indirectly through human representatives He created in His own image. Adam and Eve were to rule under God's appointment and reproduce and maintain the order and government of the Kingdom of Heaven on Earth. From the beginning, the Earth was designed to be ruled by one government—the Kingdom of Heaven. Any other government is illegal on this planet. This is why the Bible makes it clear that human governments exist only by God's permission and that He ordained them for the protection of society and the common human welfare until the day His Kingdom government on Earth is fully restored. In his letter to the believers in Rome, Paul leaves no doubt as to the true authority behind human affairs:

> *Let everyone be subject to the governing authorities, for there is no authority except that which God has established. The authorities that exist have been established by God. Consequently, whoever rebels against the authority is rebelling against what God has instituted, and those who do so will bring judgment on themselves. For rulers hold no terror for those who do right, but for those who do wrong. Do you want to be free from fear of the one in authority? Then do what is right and you will be commended. For the one in authority is God's servant for your good. But if you do wrong, be afraid, for rulers do not bear the sword for no reason. They are God's servants, agents of wrath to bring punishment on the wrongdoer. Therefore, it is necessary to submit to the authorities, not only because of possible punishment but also as a matter of conscience* (Romans 13:1–5 NIV).

Satan the pretender may believe that he runs the show and controls the governments of the Earth, but it is the King of Heaven who guides human history and destiny toward His desired ends. He raises up one power and brings down another, all in accordance with His sovereign will and purpose. Psalm 75:7 says, *"It is God who judges: he brings one down, he exalts another"* (NIV). In the Book of Isaiah, the Lord Himself declares:

> *Turn to me and be saved, all you ends of the earth; for I am God, and there is no other. By myself I have sworn, my mouth has uttered in all integrity a word that will not be revoked: before*

me every knee will bow; by me every tongue will swear (Isaiah 45:22-23 NIV).

Heaven: Earth's Only Legitimate Culture

Human empires rise and fall, but the Kingdom of God stands forever. Earthly rulers who forget or who refuse to acknowledge the One to whom they are accountable set themselves up for judgment and even destruction. Nebuchadnezzar, king of Babylon, ruled the mightiest empire the world had ever known up to that time, but even he had to learn to humble himself before the God of Heaven:

> *As the king was walking on the roof of the royal palace of Babylon, he said, "Is not this the great Babylon I have built as the royal residence, by my mighty power and for the glory of my majesty?"*

> *Even as the words were on his lips, a voice came from heaven, "This is what is decreed for you, King Nebuchadnezzar: Your royal authority has been taken from you. You will be driven away from people and will live with the wild animals; you will eat grass like the ox. Seven times will pass by for you until you acknowledge that the Most High is sovereign over all kingdoms on earth and gives them to anyone he wishes."*

> *Immediately what had been said about Nebuchadnezzar was fulfilled. He was driven away from people and ate grass like the ox. His body was drenched with the dew of heaven until his hair grew like the feathers of an eagle and his nails like the claws of a bird.*

> *At the end of that time, I, Nebuchadnezzar, raised my eyes toward heaven, and my sanity was restored. Then I praised the Most High; I honored and glorified him who lives forever.*

> *His dominion is an eternal dominion; his kingdom endures from generation to generation. All the peoples of the earth are regarded as nothing. He does as he pleases with the powers of heaven and the peoples of the earth. No one can hold back his hand or say to him: "What have you done?"*

At the same time that my sanity was restored, my honor and splendor were returned to me for the glory of my kingdom. My advisers and nobles sought me out, and I was restored to my throne and became even greater than before. Now I, Nebuchadnezzar, praise and exalt and glorify the King of heaven, because everything he does is right and all his ways are just. And those who walk in pride he is able to humble (Daniel 4:29–37 NIV).

To say that God is Lord of lords means that He owns everything there is by right of creation; to call Him King of kings is to acknowledge that His government and authority are above all others. All earthly rulers, willingly or not and consciously or not, are subject ultimately to God's sovereign authority. In the end, His will shall prevail, His purpose shall be accomplished, and His Kingdom will come on Earth as it is in Heaven. The Kingdom of Heaven is the only order that God placed on the Earth. Anything else is disorder.

When satan seized control of the dominion that rightly belonged to man, he brought disorder onto the world scene—pride, envy, greed, selfishness, hatred…and man-centered religion, which reduces the life-giving principles of God's Kingdom to empty rites, rituals, and rules.

The point of all of this is to make it clear that the culture of Heaven is the only legitimate culture for the Earth. So-called human culture, which is influenced and controlled by satan—and therefore is in conflict with the culture of Heaven—is an illegitimate culture. So we have two cultures in conflict, a cultural clash between Heaven and Earth.

Culture Problems

Anyone who pays any attention at all to human events at home or abroad knows that global society is in upheaval of unprecedented proportions. We face many global challenges that we just can't solve. The United Nations was formed after the Second World War for the purpose of preventing war. Yet in the 60 years of its existence, there have been more wars than in all the rest of recorded human history. So even our best and most well-intentioned attempt to prevent ourselves from killing each other has failed. Even worse, corruption scandals in recent years have revealed that there are those within the UN itself who have placed their own enrichment ahead of the greater good and engaged in ongoing activities that have undermined the very goals the organization is trying to achieve.

If we judge only by what we see happening around us and around the world every day, how can we help but become frustrated, discouraged, and even fearful? Who among us does not wake up in the morning, glance at the news headlines or listen to broadcast news reports, and immediately become depressed? We are all looking and dreaming and hoping and praying for a better world, aren't we? Imagine what it would be like to get up one morning and find no news of war, or genocide, or ethnic cleansing, or terrorism, or starvation, or poverty. Unfortunately, truly good news like that is an increasingly rare commodity in our world today.

Strangely enough, the single biggest cause of our problems is the very thing that was supposed to provide a solution—religion. Historically, religion has been the primary driving force behind the vast majority of global conflict. This is especially true today. Global terrorism is fueled by extremist religious ideology. In the name of Allah, radical Muslim groups such as Hamas and al-Qaida utilize violence and terror to either convert or destroy the "infidels" (unbelievers). In Iraq, Sunni and Shiite Muslims kill each other in a bloodletting unleashed by the release of years of pent-up anger, resentment, hostility, and hatred. The burning of churches in Pakistan results in the retaliatory torching of temples and mosques in India.

Religion is *not* a peaceful prospect. And religious conflict is not restricted to Islam or Hinduism or other "non-Western" religions. Christianity carries its own heavy burden of responsibility for religiously motivated conflict. The Crusades of the Middle Ages and centuries of hostility and persecution between Catholics and Protestants are two prime examples. Think of all the years that Belfast and

Northern Ireland burned with unrest and violence because Catholics and Protestants were unable to live together in peace. Denominations within the Church are like little kingdoms of their own, jockeying for position and advantage and fighting amongst themselves over theology, doctrine, and theories of church government instead of working together for the common cause of the Gospel. This is why I make a clear and unambiguous distinction between the Kingdom of Heaven and institutional Christianity as a religious entity. They are not the same.

The shrinking of our global community through telecommunications technology and the Internet has greatly accelerated the rate and intensity of culture clash. A "take-no-prisoners" war is being waged for the soul of our culture, and it is vitally important that we identify the nature of the fight. What do we do when a major news magazine runs a cover story titled "Muslims in the U.S." or we discover that mosques are popping up next to churches all over America? It is a clash of cultures. How should we respond to the debate in England over whether or not female religious devotees can wear veils in school or for driver's license photographs, even though the teachers and government officials need to be able to see their faces to identify them? It is a clash of cultures. The need to preserve democratic freedom and individual rights conflicts with the need for greater security.

What do we do when the counterculture of sexual perversion labors and lobbies vigorously to dignify and legitimize itself through legislation? How should we respond to the claim that two men or two women should be able to marry each other, and even to raise children in such a same-gender household? What do we do when we claim to believe in "family values" only to discover that society has redefined *family* to mean anything anybody at all wants it to mean? This is no time to play religious games; the very life of our culture is at stake.

What do we do when 70 bishops in a major American denomination vote to ordain an openly and active gay priest as archbishop of an entire diocese? What do we do? We can't afford to remain silent. One of the worst things in the world is for people who know what is right to remain silent in the face of wrong. We need help from beyond ourselves—help from the Creator of the Earth's original and only legitimate culture.

The Power of Culture

Culture is stronger than politics. It really doesn't matter who is in power. Politicians come and go, and governments rise and fall, but culture still remains. Culture is also more powerful than religion. One of the biggest challenges that church leaders faced during the first few centuries of the Church's existence was how to keep those who were coming into the Church out of pagan backgrounds from bringing elements of their pagan culture with them and blending these with their new faith in Christ. Even today we continue to see the enormous power of culture in the fact that many believers and Kingdom citizens display lifestyles that differ little from those of people who make no claim to be in the Kingdom.

The United States of America has a rich historical heritage of faith and even today has the highest percentage of citizens who claim to be believers (Christians) of any of the industrialized nations. Yet every year in America, 500,000 unborn babies are aborted—*legally*. The most progressive nation in the world murders half a million babies in the womb every year, and the law protects both the mothers who choose to kill their children as well as the doctors who carry out the destruction. This is insanity, yet it exemplifies the power of culture over religion in its ability to shape the thoughts, values, and beliefs of people and to influence their behavior and what they are willing to accept.

In another example, gay rights activists in America have made great strides forward in their efforts to legitimize their lifestyle through the legal process. Gay marriage is already legal in the states of Massachusetts and California, and efforts to legalize it in other states are on the rise. An increasing number of Americans—many of the same ones who claim faith in Christ—say they find nothing wrong with homosexual relationships and that gays should be afforded special "civil rights" protection under the law. Legislation has even been proposed that would make anti-gay speech or activity a hate crime.

I am not picking on America here but just illustrating the power of culture over religion—even in a nation that is still widely regarded as the most "religious" nation in the industrialized world. Similar developments are taking place in other parts of the globe. We are smarter but not wiser. We are in a pitched battle for the culture of the Earth. Most often what we assume to be issues of social, religious, or political activity are really issues of culture.

Culture is the manifestation of the collective thinking of a people. This means that whoever controls the minds of the people creates and controls the culture. Culture is also a product of law. The most effective way to change a culture is to control its laws, because whatever is instated into law eventually will become accepted as "normal" by most citizens, regardless of how they might have felt at the beginning. This is all part of the process of mind control.

Is it any surprise then that when God got ready to create a nation out of people who had been slaves for 400 years, He gave them a code of law encapsulated in the Ten Commandments? God knew that before the Israelites could become a holy nation and a people set apart for Him, He had to change their thinking. His purpose was to create a Kingdom culture on Earth by raising up a nation of Kingdom thinkers and Kingdom livers.

This is why the Bible says that the law of God is good. When we obey the law of God, we are producing the culture of Heaven. This has nothing to do with practicing a religion, but rather with instating a culture based on the law of God that will permeate and transform every part of society. Paul described what it meant to exchange the world's culture for the culture of Heaven when he wrote:

> *Do not conform to the pattern of this world, but be transformed by the renewing of your mind. Then you will be able to test and approve what God's will is—his good, pleasing and perfect will* (Romans 12:2 NIV).

To renew our minds means to take on the attitude of Christ and to understand that as believers and Kingdom citizens we have the mind of Christ (see Phil. 2:5; 1 Cor. 2:16). We need to know His mind and discern His thinking. Taking up the culture of Heaven means learning to think God's thoughts and living accordingly.

The Kingdom of God is a kingdom of the heart and mind that manifests itself in culture. The secret to expanding Heaven's culture on Earth is to change people's minds, to cultivate them like a garden, carefully seeding their minds with the thoughts, beliefs, ideals, values, and convictions of Heaven. The end result will be the transformation of an arid, spiritually barren mental landscape into a verdant and vibrant garden full of life, hope, and unlimited potential.

In contrast to the world's culture—which, reflecting the character and nature of the pretender, is a culture of desperation, discrimination, depravity, division, destruction, and death—Heaven's culture is a culture of power, provision, and possibility. This is the culture of the King, of which Paul writes:

Now to Him who is able to do immeasurably more than all we ask or imagine, according to his power that is at work within us, to him be glory in the church and in Christ Jesus throughout all generations, for ever and ever! Amen (Ephesians 3:20-21 NIV).

God wants us to become all that we can be, and He has the power to enable us to succeed.

Declaration of Independence

The Kingdom of Heaven is not a religion; it is a government and a society with a culture that is just as real as any devised by man—but even more so. That is why God issued laws for us to obey in His Kingdom. Those laws produce a lifestyle, and that lifestyle manifests in a culture, in a community that creates a society that is totally unique. This is the culture that existed in the Garden of Eden, and the culture that all Kingdom citizens are to reproduce and manifest in the "gardens" of our lives as we put the Garden Principle into operation throughout the world.

Given enough time and influence, one culture can supplant another. For example, although the vast majority of Bahamian citizens are of African descent, ours is not an African culture. Visitors to our beautiful Caribbean country notice immediately that they are surrounded by the culture of Great Britain. We drive on the left side of the road, we traditionally drink tea rather than coffee, and, for many years, dressed in a "traditional" suit consisting of short pants, long socks, a long-sleeved jacket, and long necktie. For the longest time I could not understand why we wore ties in 90-degree weather, until I visited England, where it is always cold.

During the centuries when our country was a colony of Great Britain, the cultures of these islands and of our original African heritage were completely transformed by British culture. Every vestige of African or Caribbean culture was removed until today. Although we may look like Africans, we dress like the British, speak like the British, and act like the British. Even our system of government resembles that of England. One culture transformed and supplanted another.

Anyone can identify our culture by the way we look, speak, and act. Kingdom culture should be the same way. If we are Kingdom citizens, our culture should be evident to everyone we come in contact with. Worldly culture says, "Homosexual marriage is just as valid as heterosexual marriage." Kingdom culture says, "Marriage is exclusively a male-female relationship." Worldly culture says, "Have sex as often as you like with whomever you wish without guilt and without commitment." Kingdom culture says, "Reserve sex for the marriage relationship alone, and then stay married to the same spouse for life." Worldly culture says, "Live for the moment. Watch out for 'number one,' and make sure you grab your piece of the pie." Kingdom culture says, "Live with eternity in view, treat others the way you would like them to treat you, and put the interests of others ahead of your own."

It was never God's desire or intent that there be a British culture, or an American culture, or a Bahamian culture, or a Jamaican culture, or a French culture, or a Chinese culture. He wanted a Kingdom culture, one culture throughout the entire created realm. This is why Christ taught us to pray, *"Your kingdom come, your will be done, on earth as it is in heaven"* (Matt. 6:10 NIV). God wants Earth to reflect Heaven.

Culture rests on the foundation of law. God's laws are not to restrict us but to protect us and to ensure that His culture fills the Earth. This is what Adam and Eve forgot when they chose to rebel against the King in Eden. When they ate of the one tree in the Garden that God had placed off-limits, they did more than commit personal sins for the sake of pleasure and enlightenment; theirs was an act of treason against the government of their Creator. Their disobedience was, in fact, a declaration of independence from God and His righteous, loving, and benevolent rule. Adam and Eve turned their backs on God's Kingdom in favor of setting up a regime of their own making. Unfortunately, satan the pretender illegally seized the throne, began pulling the strings, and imposed his own culture of hatred, murder, and deceit.

It is no accident, then, that one of the first recorded events in this new illegitimate kingdom was an act of brother-against-brother murder. When Cain killed his brother Abel (see Gen. 4:1–16), he was simply reflecting his culture. Today, thousands of years and millions of deaths later, brother still kills brother in every nation, city, and town on Earth. It is part of our culture.

In the beginning, Adam and Eve ruled the Garden realm through the presence of the Spirit of God. When they declared their independence, the Holy Spirit departed and returned to Heaven, the home country. Man was on his own and at the mercy of the pretender. But God loved man too much to leave him on his own and with his original destiny unfulfilled. He did not leave us to fend for ourselves, spinning through space, lost in our own confusion. He said, "They may have declared their independence, but they will never survive without Me. I'm going to return to My own earthly territory and reclaim it, and them, whom I love. I planted a Garden there once. Now I will replant

My Garden, but this time I will plant it in the hearts of My people, from where it will spread to the ends of the Earth."

Restoring What the Pretender Stole

God's purpose in re-establishing His Kingdom on Earth through the life, death, and resurrection of His Son is to dethrone the pretender, kick him out of the territory, and restore what he stole from the people he has tyrannized through the ages. If we want to know what kind of ruler satan has been in his illegal regency of the earthly realm, all we have to do is look around us at the generally deplorable state the world is in spiritually, morally, and ethically. If we want to know what the pretender's rule is like, all we have to do is review any of the abundant examples from history of despotic dictators and self-serving tyrants who raped the land, robbed its resources, and victimized its citizens for their own enrichment. If we want to understand what the pretender stole from us, all we have to do is examine the common results of human colonization. As a case in point, let's consider my own nation of the Bahamas.

As I said before, my country was a colony of Great Britain for over 200 years. We were British subjects, and the British government did everything it could to make us dress, speak, and act accordingly. They even sent a governor and other political officials to administer and enforce British law in the colony. I am not suggesting that all or even most of these people were evil or had evil intent, but their presence and work in the name of the British crown had a profound impact on the Bahamian people.

Over the course of more than two centuries, a succession of governors took away from us three important ingredients of our identity as a people and replaced them with those of the home government. The first thing the governor took away from us was our *language*. Even though most Bahamians are of African descent, we do not speak African languages or dialects. We speak "the King's English" (or the Queen's).

In the same way, when the pretender took over Adam and Eve's domain, he stole their language—our ability to communicate intimately and personally with our Creator. He took away our ability to talk to God, and as a race we have been trying desperately to get it back ever since. This is why, when we become Kingdom citizens through faith in Jesus Christ, one of first things He does is restore our original language, enabling us to talk intimately, personally, and directly to God once again in a way that is not possible outside the Kingdom.

The second thing the governor took from us was our *history*. It was his job to teach us the history of the ruling kingdom, so instead of learning about Shaka Zulu and other leaders and events of African history and heritage, we learned about King Henry VIII and his six wives. We learned about Sir Francis Drake, Queen Elizabeth, and "Bloody Mary" Tudor. We studied Shakespeare. We learned about Oliver Cromwell and about the English Civil War, and thus we lost the sense of our own history.

Likewise, when the pretender seized control, he stole our knowledge of our history as a race. We forgot who we are and where we came from. We lost any sense of awareness of the Kingdom from which we originated and of the King who fashioned us in His own image. This too was restored when Christ reestablished the Kingdom of Heaven on Earth. When we first enter the Kingdom, we come to Christ with a history of sin, rebellion, and estrangement from God. Christ takes that away and gives us a new "history" of salvation, forgiveness, joy, and peace. He restores us to our rightful place as sons and daughters of the King.

Finally, the third thing the colonial governor took from us was our *culture*. We started drinking tea with chocolates three times a day. Even though few of us had ever been to England, we began each school day waving little British flags and singing, "Rule Britannia." We sang to a queen and country we had never seen. In thousands of ways every day we were surrounded by, exposed to, taught, and indoctrinated in the ways and customs of British culture until virtually all traces of any indigenous African or Caribbean culture disappeared.

The same thing happened to humankind under the pretender's rule. The more his spirit of evil permeated human society, and the more our human hearts departed from God and His ways, the more we took on the traits of the pretender's depraved and decadent culture, and the less we remembered the righteousness, peace, joy, and abundance of the culture of Heaven. Christ came to restore all of that. When we become Kingdom citizens, He gives us a new nature to supplant our old, corrupt, sinful nature—a new nature that loves God and delights to do His will and that understands, desires, and has the power to live according to Kingdom culture.

Christ came to give us back what the pretender stole. We are talking about a complete change of culture. We cannot be in the Kingdom of God and continue to live the way we used to live. When His Kingdom takes over our lives, everything changes.

The colonial governor of the Bahamas lived in a large pink house built by the British, and when we declared our independence, he returned to England. The Governor of God's Kingdom on Earth, on the other hand, will never be evicted and sent home because He does not reside in a physical building. Acts 17:24 says, *"The God who made the world and everything in it is the Lord of heaven and earth and does not live in temples built by human hands"* (NIV). Instead, through His Holy Spirit, He dwells in the hearts and lives of the citizens of His Kingdom.

The Return of the King

One of the biggest problems most of us face as believers and Kingdom citizens is that we try to reproduce the new Kingdom culture with our old, un-renewed minds. Our minds have already been tainted and corrupted by worldly culture, which makes our efforts to create good government, promote clean living, and improve society largely ineffectual at best. It is impossible to draw fresh water from a bitter source.

When Christ came to Earth to restore His Father's Kingdom, the first thing He had to do was clean house. Before He could send His Spirit to dwell in us, He had to wash away the filth He found there—the sin, immorality, degradation, evil, bitterness, envy, jealousy, anger, deceit, gluttony, greed, sexual perversion, prejudice, hatred, and lust. His death on the cross was the cleanup program. His blood has the power to wash away all the filth and degradation of the pretender and his evil rule. Christ came to wash us free of our sins in order to prepare the "house" of our bodies for the return of the Royal Governor so that Heaven's culture—our original culture—can come back.

Jesus made it clear that restoring the Kingdom and reinstating its culture on Earth had nothing to do with buildings when He said:

> *The coming of the kingdom of God is not something that can be observed, nor will people say, "Here it is," or "There it is," because the kingdom of God is in your midst* (Luke 17:20-21 NIV).

But before the Kingdom can be within us, we must be thoroughly cleansed from the inside out so that the Holy Spirit can inhabit a holy temple. We are not talking about religion here but about the return of legitimate government. The Holy Spirit dwelling in us means that the entire government of Heaven is on the Earth today. This is what Jesus meant when He said that the Kingdom of God is within us.

The Kingdom of Heaven has been reinstated in the territory stolen by the pretender, and it will continue to gain ground. A royal Garden has bloomed in the desert and is spreading inexorably and irresistibility over the barren ground, preparing the way for the day when the King Himself will return visibly and powerfully to take His throne. At that time, the Earth will be filled with the knowledge of His glory, as the waters cover the sea (see Hab. 2:14).

The culture of God must come back to Earth. He has called us and commissioned us to make a difference in the world. It is time for Kingdom citizens everywhere to infuse this sick world with the curative elixir of the culture of Heaven. Our King has placed us here to seed worldly government with the government of the Kingdom. He has called us to invade the culture of worldly business with the business of Heaven. This is not about profit but about permeation.

Like yeast, we are to infiltrate and permeate the world with Kingdom culture until the whole is transformed—until the barren desert is a beautiful, fertile, and fruitful Garden once more.

The Kingdom of Heaven is not about escaping Earth; it is about occupying the planet. As Kingdom citizens, we are destined to change the world. In the name of Jesus the King, nations and peoples will be set free from the cruel bondage and deadly culture of satan the pretender. The time of the Kingdom of God is upon us. Let His Kingdom come. Let His will be done on Earth as it is in Heaven. Let us live according to His laws and principles. Let His culture reign supreme. Let the Earth be filled with His glory.

Living in Two Worlds on One Earth

Kingdom citizens are people with their feet in two different worlds. One foot is planted squarely in the Kingdom community—where daily life is ordered by the righteous principles, standards, and culture of God Almighty—while the other stands securely in the society and culture of the world. At heart, the two worlds are incompatible because they operate according to principles and philosophies that are diametrically opposed to each other. Yet we live in both worlds simultaneously. This is the challenge of living in the Kingdom. In order to do so successfully, we have to understand the principles of Kingdom extension and influence and how they work in conjunction with the present culture we are in. How do we live in two worlds on one Earth? More importantly, how do we claim one world—the popular culture—and bring it under Kingdom government?

Attitude is the key, and attitude determines strategy.

To begin with, we must have the proper attitude with regard to the Kingdom of Heaven and the kingdom of this world. The first is eternal, while the second is temporal. In other words, though the Kingdom of Heaven will last forever, the kingdom of this world will someday pass away to be replaced by a new kingdom on a new Earth. Psalm 45:6 says, *"Your throne, O God, will last for ever and ever; a scepter of justice will be the scepter of your kingdom"* (NIV). A king's scepter is the symbol of his power, authority, and favor. Whoever has the scepter acts in the king's authority, and the one to whom the king holds out his scepter receives the king's favor. So the scepter represents the character of the king and his rule. Justice, then, is the character of God and His Kingdom.

Psalm 103:19 says, *"The Lord has established his throne in heaven, and his kingdom rules over all"* (NIV). *All* means everything there is. There is nothing and no one anywhere over whom God does not rule. If justice is the character of God's Kingdom, then the universe in its entirety is the scope of God's Kingdom.

Psalm 145:13 says, *"Your kingdom is an everlasting kingdom, and your dominion endures through all generations"* (NIV). From eternity past to eternity future, God's Kingdom endures. If justice is the character of God's Kingdom and the universe is its scope, then eternity is its duration.

Recognizing the just, universal, and eternal nature of the Kingdom of Heaven should inspire us to adjust our attitude to acknowledge that the kingdom of this world can never equal or compete with God's eternal Kingdom. The knowledge that we are citizens of a just Kingdom that can never be overthrown and will never pass away should give us boldness as we engage the kingdom of this world and its culture.

Whenever we pray, "Your Kingdom come, and Your will be done on Earth as it is in Heaven," we are praying for the celestial to transform the terrestrial. *Celestial* means heavenly, invisible, and spiritual. As children of God created in His image and likeness, we have firm connections to both worlds. On the one hand, we are celestial, spiritual beings who will live forever, while on the other hand, our beings are housed in terrestrial, physical bodies of clay that will die and decay, only to be replaced by new bodies that will not. No other creatures in the whole of God's universal Kingdom have this dual celestial-terrestrial nature. So we are ideally suited by nature and design to be God's instruments to transform the terrestrial realm into the likeness of the celestial.

No Coexistence

One of the first attitude adjustments we must make is to get rid of our "religious" thinking. As I have stressed over and over, Kingdom living has nothing to do with religion. For one thing, religious thinking believes in coexistence; it makes room for everybody—every sect, every denomination, every belief system, every philosophy; those with high values and those with no values at all; those who believe in many gods, one god, or no god. Coexistence says, "Let's all try to get along. After all, there are many roads to the truth, and each road is just as valid as the next." Coexistence makes room for Islam, Hinduism, Buddhism, Judaism, Christianity, Christian Science, Scientology, Unitarianism, Baha'i, Hare Krishna, witchcraft, animism, atheism, and all the rest. Coexistence regards accommodation as the highest value.

There is no such thing as coexistence in the Kingdom of Heaven. The Kingdom did not come to Earth to coexist; it came to take over and transform. In the Kingdom there is only one vision, one will, one standard, one law, one belief system, one value system, one moral code, one code of ethics, one code of conduct, and one culture—the King's. The existence of any other constitutes rebellion. If the King's word is law and absolute, how can there be multitudes of little "kingdoms" within the Kingdom? There can't be. There is only one King and only one Kingdom, so coexistence is impossible.

We have already seen how Jesus likened the Kingdom of Heaven to yeast. Let's imagine for a moment that we have a large mixing bowl containing lumps of dough made from different kinds of flour—white, wheat, oat, rice, nut, etc. And let's imagine further that each of these lumps represents a "kingdom" of the world, whether a nation, a religion, or whatever. Now suppose that we mix yeast in with all those different lumps of dough. What do you think will happen? Do you think the yeast will discriminate between the different kinds of flour? Each kind of flour is different, but the yeast doesn't care; it ignores those distinctions, proceeds with its fermentation process, and transforms the entire batch of dough.

God's Kingdom is not here to coexist with the kingdoms of this world, but to supplant and transform them. A multi-faith rally in Mexico City that I attended is a case in point. That rally was organized around the philosophy of coexistence. All of the world's major religions (and many of the minor ones) were represented, and each one was afforded equal dignity, respect, and honor. All the speakers were received respectfully and politely. But when I stood up and talked about the Kingdom—not religion—everyone in the arena was clamoring for more. Why? The message of the Kingdom is like yeast in the dough of religion and worldly kingdoms. Yeast doesn't believe in coexistence. It permeates and agitates and will not stop until it has transformed its environment into something completely new. The Kingdom of Heaven cannot simply and tidily be given a place sharing the stage with all the religions, philosophies, and faith systems of the world. It will grow and expand and overwhelm and transform until it alone is left.

So all who are Kingdom citizens face the dilemma and challenge of how to live successfully and simultaneously in two worlds that are in inevitable conflict. One critical key to our successful navigation within these two worlds is to get it thoroughly into our heads that the Kingdom of Heaven is not a kingdom of coexistence but of transformation, and that it is the Kingdom, not the world, that will ultimately prevail. This understanding can help us develop the habit of thinking with a Kingdom mindset and making Kingdom decisions in every area of life.

As Kingdom citizens, we must be prepared for clash and conflict. We cannot enter the Kingdom of God and continue to live like our unsaved friends. All of a sudden everything changes: our culture, our nature, our interests, our priorities, our tastes—everything. We are new creations in Christ; the old is gone and everything has become new (see 2 Cor. 5:17). Our assignment on Earth is not coexistence, compromise, or half measures. It is total transformation. It is love taking over a love-starved planet.

Kingdom Transformation in Action

We're not talking about theoretical concepts here, but principles that actually work in practical, everyday ways. For example, there is a woman in our congregation who not long ago took over as manager of a dying restaurant, and within six months, by applying Kingdom principles, turned it completely around. One of the first decisions she made as manager was to set a standard for all the workers—a Kingdom standard. She retrained all the staff and helped re-ignite their passion for their work and for the restaurant's success. Prior to her arrival, each of the chefs cooked everything, according to what came along. She organized them according to their gifts and abilities so that each chef prepared the dishes he or she was especially good at.

The restaurant had televisions that previously had been used to watch anything. This Kingdom manager established a policy that limited the television viewing to two channels—TBN (Trinity Broadcasting Network) and CNN. No one, including the customers, was allowed to change the channels. She did this so that as manager she could control and create an appropriate atmosphere. If a customer asked to change the channel, she politely and respectfully declined, saying that she appreciated the customer's business, but that those were the rules.

Her lifestyle of uncompromising but non-belligerent obedience to Kingdom principles even in the workplace brought about a transformation in the lives of her employees. Their attitudes and morale changed drastically as they observed the consistency and excellence of her management style and operating principles. She and her employees regularly pray together, and she testifies that today there is continual worship in both the kitchen and the office. In addition, the restaurant is closed on Sundays so that all the workers can go to their own houses of worship.

When this dedicated Kingdom citizen and servant took over, the restaurant was dying. Within months, the restaurant had become so popular that customers were waiting in line even before the 11 A.M.

opening time, and on most days, from 11:30 A.M. to 3 P.M., the line is out the door. Income for the business has tripled since she became manager, enabling her to give generous raises to the employees. The business even bought one employee a car and gave computers to two of the student employees. Turnaround of workers is low, and the restaurant is now looking to expand into a franchise and even go international.

That is quite a transformation, from a single struggling restaurant to a successful and growing operation—and all because one dedicated Kingdom citizen determined to apply Kingdom principles, without compromise or coexistence, in the place where God had placed her.

Whenever the Kingdom comes into a place, it impacts and overrides the culture of that place, not with violence or heavy-handed tactics, but with love and an unshakable confidence in the absolute legitimacy, superiority, and supremacy of Kingdom government. We are not supposed to dress like the popular culture, or live like the popular culture, or take a light view of sex and morality like the popular culture. We are supposed to set the standard, the higher standard of the Kingdom. We are supposed to override the popular culture. We are supposed to exercise self-control and moderation in all things and impact the people around us. We should not allow the environment to change us.

Instead, we should change our environment and bring it into conformity with God's Kingdom. The apostle Paul said, *"Do not conform to the pattern of this world, but be transformed by the renewing of your mind"* (Rom. 12:2 NIV). Once transformed in this manner, we then transform our environment wherever we go until it is a clear reflection of the Kingdom.

No coexistence. Transformation of the popular culture will come only from communities of Kingdom citizens who refuse to remain silent, who refuse to sit idly by, uninvolved and disengaged, while the agents of the *"powers of this dark world and...the spiritual forces of evil in the heavenly realms"* (Eph. 6:12 NIV) set their agenda and run the show. We must speak up. We must step out. We must get involved. We must become proactive in reproducing Garden communities of the Kingdom wherever we are and wherever we go in the future. That is our calling and our assignment from the One who commanded us to *"go and make disciples of all nations, baptizing them in the name of the Father and of the Son and of the Holy Spirit, and teaching them to obey everything I have commanded you"* (Matt. 28:19-20 NIV).

The Kingdom We've All Been Looking For

Human history is replete with examples of good kings and bad kings, good kingdoms and bad kingdoms, benevolent governments and oppressive governments. One fact that stands out clearly is this: As the king goes, so goes the kingdom. A kingdom is tied so closely to the nature and character of its king, so it is virtually impossible for a good kingdom to come from a bad king or a bad kingdom to come from a good king. Jesus put it this way:

> *No good tree bears bad fruit, nor does a bad tree bear good fruit. Each tree is recognized by its own fruit. People do not pick figs from thornbushes, or grapes from briers. A good man brings good things out of the good stored up in his heart, and an evil man brings evil things out of the evil stored up in his heart. For the mouth speaks what the heart is full of* (Luke 6:43–45 NIV).

Fortunately for all of us, the King of kings is a good King, and His Kingdom is a good kingdom. That is why we who are citizens of the Kingdom of Heaven can live and work for the Kingdom—and engage the popular culture with it—in complete confidence that we are serving not only God, but also the better interests of our fellow humans who are not yet in the Kingdom. Our King's rule is just and righteous. He rules with fairness, grace, compassion, mercy, and, most of all, love. And in His love He delights to give all good things to His children, His people. James, the brother of Jesus, wrote, *"Every good and perfect gift is from above, coming down from the Father of the heavenly lights, who does not change like shifting shadows"* (James 1:17 NIV). Jesus Himself said, *"Do not be afraid, little flock, for your Father has been pleased to give you the kingdom"* (Luke 12:32 NIV). No matter who we are, and whether we realize it or not, the Kingdom of Heaven is the kingdom we have always been looking for.

The nature of a king and his government determines the quality of life in his kingdom. If the king is corrupt, then his kingdom will be characterized by corruption, oppression, evil, and injustice. Such was the experience of millions, including the early Christians, under the rule of Rome. The Roman Empire endured a succession of evil and depraved rulers, and the quality of life across the empire reflected it. The King of the Ages, however, rules with absolute love, beneficence, and equanimity.

In addition, the wealth of a kingdom will be reflected in the lifestyle of its people. If the kingdom is rich and the king is good, the people will be well off. If the kingdom is poor or the king corrupt, the people will live in poverty. Our Kingdom belongs to a King who owns everything. The Earth is the Lord's, and everything on it (see Ps. 24:1), and the heavens belong to Him as well (see Ps. 115:16). He bestows favor and honor and withholds no good thing from those who obey Him (see Ps. 84:11). And the apostle Paul assures us that *"God will meet all your needs according to the riches of his glory in Christ Jesus"* (Phil. 4:19 NIV). He will supply everything we need on Earth, but not necessarily from the Earth. His supply will come to us from the limitless riches of Heaven.

In other words, our needs can be met based on how much the Kingdom has. Unlimited resources mean unlimited provision. There is no lack in the Kingdom of Heaven. The meaning of Matthew 6:33 is that if we place our top priority on seeking first the Kingdom and righteousness of God, then His government will supply all of our basic necessities as a Kingdom obligation to its citizens. The King fulfills this obligation freely and willingly out of His love for us.

Finally, the quality of life of citizens of a kingdom is at the mercy of the character of the king. Jesus said:

> Come to me, all you who are weary and burdened, and I will give you rest. Take my yoke upon you and learn from me, for I

am gentle and humble in heart, and you will find rest for your souls. For my yoke is easy and my burden is light (Matthew 11:28–30 NIV).

"All" means everybody. The King has the power to give rest to everyone who comes to Him—including all 7 billion plus of us on the face of the Earth. This is not some sweet and sentimental religious statement; it is a legal Kingdom decree. "Come to Me, all 7 billion and more of you; I can heal you all, house you all, feed you all, dress you all, and bless you all—and still have as many resources as when I began."

Jesus is a good King, and His Kingdom is just what the world needs, which is why He wants to fill the Earth with His Kingdom communities and use His citizens to do it.

Victory Through Service

But how do we do it? What is our personal strategy for carrying out our King's Garden Expansion Program? We must not use the methods or ways of the world because the world's ways are at odds with the ways of the Kingdom. The world operates through self-promotion and the pursuit of selfish ambition. But the Kingdom operates by different principles. An incident involving two of Jesus's disciples gave Him the opportunity to teach all of them about greatness and advancement in the Kingdom of Heaven:

> *Then the mother of Zebedee's sons [James and John] came to Jesus with her sons and, kneeling down, asked a favor of Him.*
>
> *"What is it you want?" He asked.*
>
> *She said, "Grant that one of these two sons of mine may sit at your right and the other at your left in your kingdom."*
>
> *"You don't know what you are asking," Jesus said to them. "Can you drink the cup I am going to drink?"*
>
> *"We can," they answered.*

Jesus said to them, "You will indeed drink from my cup, but to sit at my right or left is not for me to grant. These places belong to those for whom they have been prepared by my Father."

When the ten heard about this, they were indignant with the two brothers. Jesus called them together and said, "You know that the rulers of the Gentiles lord it over them, and their high officials exercise authority over them. Not so with you. Instead, whoever wants to become great among you must be your servant, and whoever wants to be first must be your slave—just as the Son of Man did not come to be served, but to serve, and to give his life as a ransom for many" (Matthew 20:20–28 NIV).

"Not so with you." With these words Jesus clearly and permanently distinguished Kingdom life and ways from those of the world. In the world, kings and rulers vaunt their authority over others. "Not so with you." In the world, officials and others in power exercise authority over others, often in selfish or oppressive ways. "Not so with you." In the world, people put themselves forward, scrambling over or pulling down anyone who gets in their way in their struggle to become top dog. "Not so with you."

Greatness and success in the Kingdom come not through self-promotion and ambitious positioning, but through self-abasement and servanthood. By self-abasement I do not mean false modesty or humility, or becoming a pushover or a doormat for people to walk all over. Self-abasement means a genuinely humble spirit that regards selfless service to others in the name of the King as the greatest honor and privilege that anyone could be given. As sinners who were once in rebellion against God, we deserve nothing from Him except judgment and condemnation. Yet God, in His great mercy and love, forgave our sins through Christ, brought us into His glorious and eternal Kingdom, and assigned us to represent His Kingdom on Earth, even as we enjoy all its benefits. What greater privilege could there be?

"Not so with you." Our culture is different. We don't do things the way the rest of the world does. In the world, people seek greatness through money, power, and the praise and admiration of others.

Jesus said that they have their reward (see Matt. 6:2). Greatness in the Kingdom of God comes through service, the selfless giving of ourselves for the benefit of others. If our King came to serve rather than to be served, how can we do anything different?

Find Your Gift and Serve It to the World

"The Son of Man did not come to be served, but to serve, and to give his life as a ransom for many" (Matt. 20:28 NIV). Notice the progression here: Jesus became a servant, and then He gave Himself. By His example He is telling us: "Find your gift and serve it to the world. That is how you will infect people with the Kingdom." If you set your heart on the Kingdom of Heaven and your sights on serving others in the King's name, He will open doors of opportunity for you that would never open otherwise. He will take you to places you would never be able to go on your own and enable you to impact lives you would never even come close to touching any other way. He will take you to personal heights of joy, prosperity, and contentment beyond your wildest dreams and give you a broader influence in your world than you have ever imagined. But those things come not by seeking them, but by seeking Him; not by seeking the gifts, but by seeking the Giver.

Jesus said that *whoever* wants to become great in the Kingdom must become a servant. "Whoever" means that greatness in the Kingdom is available to anyone—anyone willing to pay the price, that is. And what is the price? It is setting aside your own will and ambitions and offering yourself willingly as a servant—even a slave—of the King. It is giving up your right to yourself in complete surrender to the will and purpose of God, to go where He says to go and to do what He says to do.

Everyone dreams of being great, and there is nothing evil in that desire. We all want to be part of something significant. This is perfectly natural. Such a desire comes from God, because He created us for greatness, but we lost it when we lost the Kingdom. We can get it back, but not by walking on top of people, pushing people down, lording it over people, conniving, scheming, lying, stealing, or dealing under the table. Those are the ways of the world. In God's country, if you want to be great, you first must become the servant of all.

What Jesus was actually saying is that when we become servants of the King, we are supposed to serve something to the world. If we want to become great, we have to find our gift, refine it, and serve it to the world, not for our sake but for the world's, and for the sake of our King and His great name.

There is actually a process. First, you must find your gift; discover it. Second, you must define your gift; understand it. Third, you must refine your gift; begin using it in small ways faithfully, and in larger ways as the Lord gives you opportunity. This means distributing your gift for free, giving it away. Slaves don't receive pay for their labors; they work for free. But as you serve humbly and faithfully, giving freely of yourself, the King will be watching and will reward you. As you prove yourself faithful in little things, He will entrust you with greater things.

So keep on laboring faithfully in the men's ministry, or the children's ministry, or the music ministry, or the soup kitchen, or wherever God has placed you and however He has gifted you. Set your heart on the Kingdom, serve your gift to the world, and be faithful; and eventually God will elevate you in some way. You have to become a slave of your gift, for when you serve your gift, you are serving yourself to others. The more you give of yourself, the greater you will become in the eyes of those you serve, because they will see in you the image, likeness, and heart of the King.

God's big idea was to extend His kingly influence and culture from the celestial to the terrestrial by planting Garden communities throughout the Earth that would perfectly reflect the richness and abundant Life of His heavenly Kingdom. And He chose to do it through citizen-servants like you and me who will seek first His Kingdom and His righteousness and live exclusively for Him. We do this by humbling ourselves and giving ourselves freely to others so that they may see Him in us, learn of His Kingdom from us, and apply for citizenship themselves. Let us be faithful to our calling and hasten the day when *"the earth will be filled with the knowledge of the glory of the Lord as the waters cover the sea"* (Hab. 2:14 NIV).

Glossary of Terms That Change the Conversation

Ambassador-kings: The ambassadors of the King are far more than the traditional word *ambassador* implies. It would be a big mistake to try to define their roles in any terms that are familiar. They are far more involved, far more engaged, and far more effective than can be understood by conventional terminology. Their lives carry a peace, their voice an assurance. Their policy positions are authentic, their words are genuine, and their wisdom indisputable. They carry the authority of the King, for the King lives His Life through the ambassador-king.

Ancients: The collective voice of the Hebrew prophets who spoke of current events as far back as ancient Egypt.

Assured Domination: This is the term to describe the goal of any organization—that is, to secure their rule and authority generationally. Their plan is generational, planning and executing modest gains within a set of smaller time frames. The control of education, media, entertainment, and religion makes it easier to keep their ideology embedded in the hearts and minds of the population and at the forefront of popular thought.

Authority: Authentic *authority* cannot be imparted. It cannot be assigned, demanded, or assumed. Authority is earned in the crucible of living, where Brokenness requires obedience while our humanity screams for attention. The repentant surrender of the human ways of self-serving agendas releases the power of the King's Life that will emerge from within. His authority reigns when their surrender is unconditional and consistent. "It is no longer I who live, but Christ lives in me" (Gal. 2:20).

Broken: Death to self-rule and coming alive to the rule of the King. This is the condition of the heart of a person who has surrendered to their Lord. A broken person is one who is soft, pliable, and dependent on his Lord. He has wrestled with God and walks with a limp of painful remembrance of his resistance to God's Life within him. This is a coveted condition in God that we all have ample opportunity to experience. This should not be confused with the works of evil men who kill, steal, and destroy the hope, joy, and dreams of a believer. True spiritual brokenness is ultimately empowering, faith building, and destiny releasing. "Weeping may last for the night, but a shout of joy comes in the morning" (Ps. 30:5).

Brokenness: Most of us think we know what brokenness is; that is why we run from it. Brokenness is a companion that, when allowed to journey with us, teaches, strengthens, encourages us daily along the way. Brokenness is with us primarily to remind us that He is within us, that there is nothing random, nothing that is meaningless to our lives. Brokenness assures us that He is intimately involved with all our activities. She teaches us that we are securely in God's hands, that God is working every circumstance for our good and the good of His Kingdom. Yes, Brokenness will want us to endure hardship with a right attitude, face injustice with peace, and refuse discouragement when things don't happen the way we want them to. Brokenness has a one-track mind— God's dream for us, fulfilled here and now.

Comfort Zone: It is a way of thinking, a way of living, a way of believing that protects our way of life as we know it, as we want it right now. Most dangerous is the belief that we have arrived—that we have been tried, broken, and now rest in the place of perfect abandonment to Him. Comfort zones, by definition, assume there is nothing more to personally learn, discover, and experience. It says we are quite happy where we are and that life could not get any better than it is right now. Every serious disciple of Christ should understand that there are greater adventures that await if we are willing to walk further than our current comfort zones allow.

Conscious Awareness: This lifestyle of conscious awareness of the King's Presence is unique indeed. It is an incredible combination of brokenness and power, weakness and resolve, doubt and confidence, fear and assurance. His Presence reflects absolute dependence on Him and absolute certainty of His Life pulsing through the believer's spiritual veins. It is exhilarating and frightful, natural and very much supernatural, manifesting through meekness but unlimited in love and power. The awareness of His manifest Presence is not a gift; it is the product of broken repentance.

Die: This is a spiritual term that is not always well received or understood. To die is to surrender your will to the will of the King that He might increase His Kingdom authority in your heart. John said, "He must increase, but I must decrease" (John 3:30). To "die to myself" is the key to reigning in this life in all you do. In dying to self, we live to the King. That is, His Life replaces ours, His will replaces ours, His love and compassion rises and overtakes our thoughts and actions toward everyone.

Discernment: Unfortunately, true spiritual discernment is rare indeed. Our beliefs are formed by doctrine, political correctness, culture, politics, and religious assumption. It's easy to get direction with this kind of shallow, intellectual "discernment." True discernment can differentiate between the Presence of the Lord and anything that comes from another source. Discernment means one can understand the heart of God without outside influence. True discernment also separates the holy from the unholy. True spiritual discernment is a product of the Mountain of the House of the Lord and trumps everything that opposes the truth.

Now therefore, O kings, show discernment; take warning, O judges of the earth. Worship the Lord with reverence (Psalm 2:10-11).

And this I pray, that your love may abound still more and more in real knowledge and all discernment, so that you may approve the things that are excellent, in order to be sincere and blameless until the day of Christ (Philippians 1:9-10).

Divine: The Godhead. In this book, the Divine IS God. Normally used to describe something otherworldly, mystical or unexplainable. The word historically separates the reality of God and places His attributes in an undefinable category.

Evidence: A tree will flourish where it is properly planted, watered, and fed. That same tree will reveal its usefulness by producing the evidence of the fruit that it bears. The kind of tree and its purpose is determined by the fruit that grows from its branches. A tree may be lush in branches and leaves, it may be beautiful to look at, even majestic in appearance, but to earn a place it must produce evidence of its kind.

Fleshy: Base, human instinct that demands its own way, its own answers, and its own control. A fleshy person will resist the needs of others, their opinions, and their goals. That same person will resist God by whatever excuse he can get his own heart to believe.

Fruit-proof: The true priesthood of the believer, the great Melchizedek of God, is like a tree. The Bible calls them "trees of righteousness." Like a tree in an orchard, these trees of righteousness are known not by their regal appearance, not by the words that flow eloquently from their lips, but from the fruit that grows and flourishes from their lives. Jesus cursed a tree that claimed to be a fig tree but produced no figs. This fruit-proof is what separates trees that fulfill their function and those that do not. I may not be able to distinguish the difference between trees by their leaves, but I certainly know an apple from a pear from a cherry from a fig. In the last analysis, it is the fruit we bear that is proof of the kind of tree we are or are not.

God-man: Neither all man nor all God, this is the New Creation in Christ. It is the physical manifestation of the King on earth. This God-man is not Christlike; he is Christ-yielded. The human side of this person dies daily as the King died for the man. Their union is a creation of Life unseen in the earth. "If anyone is in Christ, he is a new creature [new species]; the old things passed away; behold, new things have come" (2 Cor. 5:17).

Hate: The attitude that prevents a person from fulfilling their potential. Love empowers potential; hate thwarts it. Hate is not an excuse to marginalize, separate, murder, or destroy. Hate, under any banner, is anti-King, anti-Golden Rule, anti-Life.

Hero: One who lives and loves above and beyond what is expected; performs by inner desire to do what is right consistently; a natural at putting the needs of others above his own needs.

Inclusive: Now here is a word whose definition belies those who champion it. *Inclusive* is a term that has historically meant the inclusion of all people regardless of beliefs, gender, religion, or race. But for some, *inclusive* refers to those who agree with them, whilst excluding those with whom they disagree. *Inclusive* has become that politically correct word that means very little to political ideologues who have written it across their forehead as a banner of elitism and intellectualism. But here is the honest-to-God truth: One cannot be inclusive without love. For true love overcomes differences of shape, color, religion, and, yes, even politics. Love overpowers the thing in us that wants us to separate, accuse, malign, and destroy. I know not all Christians are "inclusive." But then, not many have had an authentic encounter with the King. For those who experience Him within, *inclusive* is a way of life. Remember, you will know them by their fruit.

If I have all faith, so as to remove mountains, but do not have love, I am nothing. And if I give all my possessions to feed the poor, and if I surrender my body to be burned, but do not have love, it profits me nothing. Love is patient, love is kind and is not jealous; love does not brag and is not arrogant, does not act unbecomingly; it does not seek its own, is not provoked, does not take into account a wrong suffered, does not rejoice in unrighteousness, but rejoices with the truth; bears all things, believes all things, hopes all things, endures all things. Love never fails (1 Corinthians 13:2–8).

Influence: One can quickly tell those who influence others and those who do not. Those who influence others are not merely repeating the talking points of a particular group or movement. They speak as they, themselves, have researched, experienced, lived. These are the voices that change a culture. They are strong in their positions and can articulate their views with new insight, refreshing thought, and calm, peaceful assurance. Those who do not influence but are the victims of suppressive influence live in the shadows of yesterday, of religion, of tradition, of a politically correct—which is to say, *politically obsolete*—mindset whose goal is to cement society in a way of thinking that can be controlled and manipulated.

And do not be conformed to this world, but be transformed by the renewing of your mind, so that you may prove what the will of God is, that which is good and acceptable and perfect (Romans 12:2).

*"Behold, the former things have come to pass, now I declare **new** things; before they spring forth I **proclaim** them to you." Sing to the Lord **a new song**, sing His praise from the end of the earth!* (Isaiah 42:9-10)

Inner governance: The rule of the heart; the inner seat of authority; the things within that we submit to, believe. In the simplest terms, we are ruled by what is in our heart. We are ruled by what we give permission to rule us. Whether the rule is by religion, government, emotions, another person, our fears, or prejudices, inner governance is the inner foundational influence and control of life.

King of the Mountain of the Lord: He who reigns over the Kingdom of God. His palace is in the hearts of those who give Him access, permission within. His Name is King Jesus.

Kingdom Inner Governance: This term is in reference to the rule of the King within; the leadership of the King with His principles, His attributes, and His goals. Those under this governance are the ambassadors of the Kingdom that is established within the heart of the individual. The attributes of the King confirm the presence of the King's inner rule.

Life: The presence of God. It indwells the willing heart and flows through those who love freely. "Life" is the essence of Deity so must be capitalized when referring to His Presence.

Love: Love without legalism, commitment without control, fullness without fear, relationship without religion—the very mention of such possibilities brings feelings of exhilaration and hope, for they are the deepest yearnings of our souls. They are the essence of true love. But these passions of the heart are so foreign to the man-made rules we have been taught that to risk harboring such intimate thoughts borders upon heresy. Yet that is the peril of true love. That is the inevitable price of desire. The invasion of true love into the heart of any human being turns that person into someone quite extraordinary indeed. For nothing, nothing will ever be the same again. Nothing else will satisfy as it once satisfied; nothing else will ever be worth living for.

Manifest, manifested, manifestation: Visible to one or more of the five senses; spiritual awareness is not needed when the spirit world is manifest, or visible, recognizable by one or more of our natural senses. When God is manifest, He is recognizable in time and space, our dimension. When He is manifest in a believer, the fruit of God's Life is visible to others who do not have spiritual senses.

Melchizedek: There were three orders of priests in ancient Israel's faith. Aaron was the priesthood of the outer part of the Temple. Levi was the priesthood in charge of the center part of the Temple. Melchizedek was the priesthood of the Inner Court, the Most Holy Place, where God dwelled in manifested (always visible to the natural senses) glory. Under the New Covenant, all believers are of this inner-court priesthood. They work in His manifest Presence. This priesthood actually is the Most Holy Place, the dwelling place of God and of the King in manifest glory for all to see. Melchizedek is known for his way of life, not for his words. His ministry is in the Presence of God. Melchizedek's brokenness allows the King to express Himself through this priesthood.

Mountain of the House of the Lord: This is not a religious mountain. It is a spiritual mountain of governance. It is the bedrock of the King's authority and established in the hearts of those who surrender to His inner governance. This authority cannot be imposed upon another. It is established in the heart as each person will. When folks with the King's inner governance are together, the Kingdom is seen on earth. The Ancients called it Mount Zion, the place the King lived.

New Vocabulary: The words and concepts that move the attitudes and thoughts to a new way of thinking. Those who establish a new vocabulary into the culture eventually set policy.

Outer governance: The rule of man imposed by another; forced control of actions, attitudes, activities, and beliefs by a person, religion, or government without a corresponding, voluntary, inner change.

Paradigm Shift: A total change of thinking as evidenced by change in actions, policy, governance.

Policy: A King's decree born out of the King's decision.

Presence: Ancient Israel had a daily experience of God's Presence. Their enemies feared them because His Presence was with them. Ancient Israel had a King unlike any other nation for their King was with them. Their enemies knew that the Presence of Israel's God among them would spell doom for those who fought them. When the angels announced the birth of Jesus, they called Him *Emanuel,* which is to say, "God is with us." Jesus's coming was to assure the perpetual victory of His people, for His Presence would be within them forever. He is in us—not vicariously, not symbolically, not temporally, not dependent upon my feelings on a certain day. His Presence is within us. Period. Your success is not in political prowess; it is not in talent, in intelligence, in connections, or in hard work. *God is with us.* His Presence has taken up permanent residence within. *This* makes the enemies of our soul tremble— nothing else. The Presence of God is rising in His people.

Religion: Humanity's attempt at reaching God; a rule of man-made laws and customs designed to keep the people under the control of its leaders with little regard for their personal and spiritual welfare.

Repent: More than a desire to change actions, to repent means to determine to change actions. To turn from one way of living to another.

Species Aware: Physical, emotional, and spiritual connection with the species of which one is a part; understanding the role of every individual of the species and the knowledge of their interconnectedness and their reliance upon one another.

Spiritual outsourcing: The repetitive proclamations of things discovered long ago as though they were new; being an echo and not the voice.

Spiritual DNA: Just as your natural DNA tells the unchangeable story of who you are physically and emotionally, your spiritual DNA tells you who you are in Spirit. It is the locked truth of what God made you to be and the destiny that is His plan for your life.

Secularist: One who considers the answers to human ills to come from science, intellectualism, psychology. Secularists do not see a spiritual element to the health of the human condition.

Statesman: A person of integrity to the core of his being; a person who sees the best in everyone; encourages, empowers, and enlightens folks; one who has the best interests of all humanity at heart.

Surrender: To yield to another; to relinquish control in order to embrace another's rule, authority, or way of life; to replace your will for the will of another to the point that it is obviously evident to those around you as well as yourself.

Tolerant: The emotional ability to allow another to live, believe, function according to his own set of morals though they differ from your own. God does not call us to be tolerant. He calls us to love and to love beyond our own attitudes and personal feelings. That's why John said "He must increase, but I must decrease." He does not want us shoving our negative feelings deep inside ourselves. He wants us to die to them. Then we are not tolerant; we love naturally. Today's tolerant folks merely hide their real feelings and present a façade. No one wants to think folks are just tolerating them. They want to be accepted, loved, appreciated. Tolerance is a deception that only works until something comes up that is so against what you feel that your true feelings come blurting out. Obviously, then, there is no consistency in tolerance. It is a fleshy, deceptive way of looking pious, but at best it is only temporary.

Within: Your inner consciousness, your will, your inner seat of governance. This is where we really live. This is where the real *you* hangs his hat. Many believe that the King lives within, but their lives rarely reflect the Presence of a reigning King. If we truly believe that the King is within and He is building His Kingdom within, life would certainly be very different than it is now.

Word Become Flesh: The process of our words, our belief systems becoming a natural part of our lives. Spiritual transformation results in the super-"natural" lifestyle of the attributes of the King.

About Don Nori, Sr.

Don Nori, Sr. is a driven man. The same passion for Jesus that arrested him over forty years ago is the passion that led him to start Destiny Image Publishers in 1983 and is still the primary overshadowing power in his life today. Along with Cathy, his wife of more than 43 years, they pursue life enthusiastically in the beautiful Cumberland Valley of central Pennsylvania. They spend much of their time happily spoiling their grandchildren and enjoying their sons and their wives. Don will probably write as long as God gives him breath.

About Dr. Clyde Rivers

Dr. Clyde Rivers is the Honorary Ambassador at Large for the Republic of Burundi, Africa. He is the founder and CEO of iChange Nations and works as a world peace ambassador for Golden Rule International. He is the senior pastor of Miracle Faith Church in Victorville, California, where he lives with his wife of 21 years, Maryalice.

THE
FORGOTTEN
MOUNTAIN

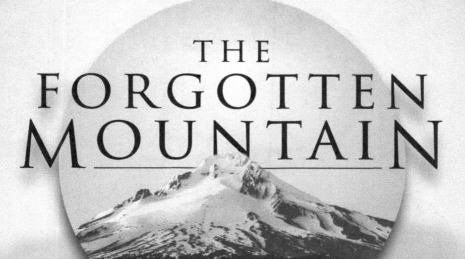

TRILOGY

The Forgotten Mountain
— BOOK ONE —

There is a reason believers struggle more than they should. There is a reason that there is so much pain, loss and heartache. It is not because we are destined to suffer because we are not. It is because we have forgotten the Mountain of the House of the Lord, the place of true inner governance under the rule of our King. He must increase and we must decrease. The Canaan lifestyle is waiting as surely as it was waiting for ancient Israel to cross the river Jordan. We reign when we die...to ourselves.

After Pentecost
— BOOK TWO —

When ancient Israel fled the bondage of Egypt, they found solace in the wilderness. But it did not last long. They wandered in the waste places and wondered why it had to be so. But it didn't have to be so. They were called to pass through the wilderness as we are called to pass through Pentecost into our Canaan in this life. Who will have the courage to leave the familiar, the secure, the visible evidence of His presence, opting for the authentic inner governance of the King; the establishing of the permanent throne of His Kingdom within?

An Uncommon Revival
— BOOK THREE —

The lifestyle of the believer in Canaan is far different from the lifestyle of the wilderness that the ancient Israelites experienced. It is also far different from the life experienced in Pentecost. In this dimension of life, the King reigns, His presence tangible from within and the attributes of the King flow like water from the surrendered life. Here, destiny is fulfilled, the contribution of every man is appreciated and authentic Divine harmony begins to flourish among men.